Open to Ideas

ROSE WEINTRAUB

Copyright © 2023 Rose Weintraub

To request permissions, contact the publisher at twosedona@yahoo.com

ISBN Paperback: 979-8-9854719-0-8
ISBN eBook: 979-8-9854719-1-5

First paperback edition April 2023

Edited by Kate Fitzgerald and Nicole Bokat

Cover Art by Lumious Antonio

Cover and interior design: Andy Meaden meadencreative.com

Printed by Draft2Digital in the USA

DEDICATION

I dedicate this book to all those who grieve and have suffered a loss.

I know how difficult it is to continue on…

but try to maintain hope that life will eventually get better.

Feel your grief and keep moving forward.

You are not alone – many of us know how you feel.

CONTENTS

ACKNOWLEDGEMENTS

I would like to thank all those who aided me in getting *Open to Ideas* published. My editors, Kate Fitzgerald and Nicole Bokat, who helped me to find my voice. Abby Heraud and David Emmons for bolstering my social media and making it far less scary to navigate. Andy Meaden for his creativity in cover design and interior book formatting and layout. Luminous Antonio for her fabulous art work, friendship and constant encouragement to write my story. Lynnda Pollio for her enduring support throughout the last few years as I tentatively moved toward publishing my book.

I particularly want to thank my step-kids, Craig and Meredith. who have lovingly kept me in their lives after their father passed. Through them, I see my beloved Mickey. In their children, Jaiden, Sam, CaiLyn and Alex, I see their grandfather. Although they never got to know Mickey very well because he died when they were so young, I believe that Mickey's spirit lives on in them.

INTRODUCTION

Journey through the Fire

My husband Mickey died when he was 63 years old, and I was 55.

It was only six months from the first "twinge" that he felt in his belly until his death. Cancer took hold of him like a rabid dog and didn't let go. His demise shook me to the core. My emotions were so close to the surface that I didn't have much control over where or when they would release—they'd often bubble up without warning.

Like many people, Mickey and I had our lives planned out. We had lots of friends, a large family, and intentions to build a dream home in Sedona, Arizona for retirement. After his death, all the plans were tossed into the air and I had to figure out what to do with my life.

I felt desperately alone. The beautiful person with whom I had shared everything was gone. Every day I awoke to face a wall of despair. The world as I knew it had begun to fade away—friends disappeared, phone calls stopped, routines altered.

I searched for answers: Why did he die? Where did he go? Questions about the meaning of life flooded my thoughts. How do I live my life? How do I manage on my own? I was thrown into a new life—a life I didn't want or expect. It was agonizing.

However, new experiences and new friends found their way to me in unexpected ways. As I became closer to these friends, they introduced me to a new way of thinking and being. I had never been a religious or spiritual person. In fact, I regularly dismissed any notion of exploring things beyond myself as being whacky and "woo-woo." Yet somehow, with the help of many, I found myself on a path of self-discovery.

For the first time, I became aware of the existence of spiritual teachers, healers, intuitives, and mediums. Although I had known about astrologers,

I had never given them much credibility. I was surprised to find that there is an exacting science behind astrology. Some people call it "New Age" thought, but I see it as "Old Age" because it's been around for centuries. Through the support of many of these people, I started moving through my grief, slowly but surely. Yes, I went through all the stages—denial, anger, bargaining, depression, acceptance. I felt every one of them... deeply. Grief is something that you go through, not something you get over—and everyone goes through their grief in their own way.

Journaling was one method that became a valuable tool for me to express and integrate my feelings. The following pages are based on my journal entries, and illustrate my way of coping, my way of experiencing. Sometimes, I think as human beings, we feel that when we approach a certain age, we will have all the answers, and things will be easier. That has not been my finding. I don't have all the answers, and life has not necessarily gotten easier. But it has gotten better. And there is always something to learn. Many of us seek to attain meaning and purpose in our lives. I was able to find it with the help of my spiritual teachers, my family, and friends. They walked with me through the fire and into the light.

Open to Ideas

1
DEVASTATION

Kansas City 2007

The room was terribly quiet. A few tearful family members, Mickey's children, Craig and Meredith, and their spouses, Jenn and Blaine, talked in hushed tones while I sat alone, near the bed, searching Mickey's face for signs. How I longed to look into his eyes just one more time. I gently touched his hand, but he was unresponsive.

The IVs and the respirator had been taken away. His erratic heartbeat crawled across the monitor—fast then slow, fast then slow, a drone of beep, beep, beep... .

The waiting was excruciating.

Conflicting feelings washed over me—part of me wanting it to be over, and part of me desperately not wanting my husband's life to end. I thought of all the beautiful times we had spent together: places we had traveled; dear friends we had made; and most importantly, the joy of watching his children grow into adults, marry, and have their own children. But I was overcome by a deep sadness, knowing that his grandchildren would be denied his presence in their lives – ball games, dance recitals, concerts, graduations, big hugs and sweet kisses.

I thought about my nursing career, how I had been at the bedside of many dying patients; I had comforted them, did what I could to ease their pain, consoled loved ones—now here I was and it was my husband I was watching as he moved towards death.

I leaned closer to Mickey, and did whatever possible to make him more comfortable: adjusting his bed covers; placing a cool cloth on his forehead; brushing his cheek. I knew that I was also trying to ease my own anguish, doing anything to keep my heart from shattering.

I softly caressed his warm, moist forehead, stroked his hair, and rested my fingers there. Several strands had fallen onto his pillow. Mickey had always been so pleased of his thick, brown, wavy locks. As he aged, he had prided himself in acquiring streaks of silver while most of his friends had started to bald.

His still, fragile hands rested on the blanket. This once robust man had withered away from 230 to 150 pounds. He was so thin that I had to remove his wedding ring from his finger as it had become too loose.

I whispered, "I love you" through my tears and froze in place. If I stayed still long enough, eternity might pass. To consider leaving was unthinkable, since after today, I would never see my Mickey alive again.

There was a sudden drop in his heart rate—slower, slower, then nothing. Standing up, I peered at the monitor. No, please… He had flat-lined just like in a movie. After several difficult hours of constant alerts, now, there was only a long, continuous whine. The nurse rushed in and switched off the monitor. I had done that so many times during my nursing career, but being at the bedside of my husband as it happened was devastating.

The room went silent, like turning off the TV in the middle of the night. Click.

He was gone.

A tremble started in my chest and spread through my arms and legs until my whole body was shaking. It felt like a roof had caved in on me and I was suffocating under the weight of it. I couldn't move. Bursting into uncontrollable tears, I collapsed into my chair. Although his death was inevitable, there had been nothing to prepare me for such finality. I kept wondering, "Is he really gone?" I put my cheek on his and sobbed. "I'm sorry; I'm so sorry Mickey. I tried to save you, but I couldn't." Meredith lovingly and gently took me by the shoulders and pulled me away.

"I don't want to go. Please, I can't go," I repeated.

"It's time," she said.

Somehow, I was able to get up and began to move towards the door. It was agonizing. Mickey and I had been together for the past sixteen years. I had done everything feasible to care for him and make things better. I wasn't ready to let him go.

We filed out one by one—reverentially with heads bent. I needed to be alone yet could not bear the thought of it. The prospect of facing the people waiting outside was overwhelming. Meredith guided me to a quiet room , sat me in a chair to be alone, and make some phone calls to my family before going out to the waiting room. The stillness was unnerving. "Now what?" I asked myself.

I was still trembling when I finally dialed the phone to reach out to my sister, Carol. She had been anticipating my call. "Please let everyone in the family know he is gone." I could scarcely believe the words that left my mouth. I was numb, drifting in space.

"Oh, Rose," Carol said. "I'm so sorry."

My mind was blank. "Will you come here soon; will you come to the funeral?" was all that I could manage to say.

"Of course we will come. I'll see which of our sisters can come."

I said thank you and hung up. The feelings I was going through were so strange. I couldn't think straight and I was still trembling all over my body.

I knew that I had to acknowledge the large group of family and friends that were packed into the waiting room. I knew that they would mean well as they tried to comfort me with their sincere condolences. I knew that I wanted to run in the opposite direction and simply return to my life, as it had been.

It was beyond my comprehension why anyone would try to engage in conversation at a time like this. But in a fog, I slowly walked out to greet those who had been keeping an all-day vigil, anticipating the unavoidable ending. I was struck by the outpouring of love and yet indifferent to it, having no idea what to say or do. People hugged me and uttered, "I'm sorry." Attempting to raise my arms to reciprocate, my grief rendered me incapable. It was as if an unseen force guided me from person to person. I put one foot in front of the other, moving forward. Little did I realize at the time that this would be a powerful and significant metaphor for my life.

2
ABOUT MICKEY

Kansas City

I met Mickey in Kansas City when he was in his late 40's. He was handsome and athletic and full of charm. One of his great joys was to ride his bicycle about town and immerse himself in the bustle of the city. After we dated for a while, he bought me a bike, bike shorts, shoes, and gloves so that I could join him on his jaunts through the streets. Whether we rode with other people or alone, invariably an adventure ensued. We moved from place to place as a couple, but wherever we landed, we put lots of miles on our trusted bikes.

Mickey delighted in talking about the days of his youth. He was an only child and the love of his parents' lives. At first, his father wasn't interested in having children, but his mother's wishes won out, and eventually, their darling Mickey came into the world. His full name was Leonard Michael (Mickey) Weintraub, named after his uncle Lazer. He often spoke about growing up Jewish in public school at a time when Jewish people were not always seen in a favorable light. Philadelphia, PA was Mickey's hometown.

He was never bullied because he had a rather large build, was very handsome, and a talented athlete. The girls paid him a lot of attention, and when the guys got to know him and learned of his religion they would say, "You're Jewish?" He'd respond indifferently, "Yeah, so?" And they would just leave him alone.

Mickey's first love was baseball. He played whenever and however he could. Although he was supposed to be attending Hebrew lessons once a week, in preparation for his Bar Mitzvah, he would run in the front door with his mitt hidden among his books, then run out the back door straight to the ball field. He always laughed that his Bar Mitzvah took place in his rabbi's office. His parents couldn't really afford a big celebration for him, but he was fine with that. After all, he hadn't learned much Hebrew.

He grew up in a three-story walkup in a poor downtown section of the city. The Weintraubs were a working-class family without luxuries, but he never spoke of feeling deprived. His dad sold shoes and his mother worked in a dress shop to make ends meet. He appreciated the company of many relatives living in the same area and boasted about being in a "cousins club" that provided all sorts of good-natured mischief. He developed a strong connection to his "Tanta" Louise, as she lived with them for a time while she went to school. He was as fond of his aunt as she was of him. He often told stories of Louise studying at her desk, how he would want her to hold him. Mickey would try to speak Yiddish to her but always pronounced the words incorrectly. Louise always found that funny.

Regardless of differences of race and religion in the neighborhood, it was a tight-knit community. The local kids would play ball all the time; they'd play catch, step ball, wall ball, and when the ball wore out, they would play half ball. At some point they'd have to figure out a way to get a new one. They were always together, either in the alleyway or in the street in front of the house—playing ball. Mickey had many friends during his time in school. One in particular, Marvin, would be a life long friend. Marvin moved to Philadelphia, and Mickey to KC, but they always remained very close friends.

Toward the end of high school, Mickey was awarded a baseball scholarship to a small college in Iowa. He was a city boy, knew nothing about Iowa, and wasn't the greatest student. So, he decided that college wasn't the best choice for him. Being the outgoing and friendly person he was, he looked for a job where he would have contact with the public and got one selling men's clothing in a department store. He was lucky enough to be hired to do some modeling. Clothing salesmen often visited the shop and he admired the way they carried themselves, and dressed in nice shoes and suits. He wanted to be like them, so decided that's what he would do for a living. He applied for a position with a company in Philadelphia and was hired to sell Bill Blass clothing. It would be a career that would last him until his retirement.

Mickey would often say, "I didn't go to college; I went to the school of hard knocks" and "I'm street smart, not book smart." Despite his quips, he was diligent about reading newspapers and watching TV to make sure that he was up on current events and, of course, sports. He was very conscious of being able to carry on a knowledgeable conversation with his friends and family and not appear to be ignorant—which he certainly wasn't.

One of his favorite stories was about how he came to live in Kansas City. His company had expanded and needed to have a presence throughout the country. They offered Mickey a territory based in Kansas City. "Where?" he said. "Look on a map it's in the heart of the USA," his boss encouraged. He loved Philadelphia; but he must have been ready to leave, so he took the job. Colleagues at the store teased, "What did you do that was so bad that they're sending you to, where—Kansas City?" But it would prove to be one of the best decisions he would ever make. He had recently gotten married to his girlfriend Cindy; so he and his new bride packed up and headed west. As it turned out, he would live in the Kansas City area for over thirty years and during those years he would have two children, Craig and Meredith, and make new friends—many of whom he considered to be family. Several of the friends Mickey and Cindy met in KC had moved from the East Coast also, so there was a special bond between them and enduring relationships. They began having children at the same time so the kids all grew up together and referred to the parents as Aunt and Uncle, a wonderful extended family.

As the years went on, a few of the couples got divorced. Mickey and Cindy divorced in the mid 1980's

I met Mickey in 1989 on a blind date. It would be the best date in my life.

Journal Entry
JANUARY 15, 2008

Sedona

It's been one month since Mickey died. I still can't believe it. Sorrow and grief ooze out of my pores. I keep waiting for a phone call— there are so many things I want to tell him. Maybe he's just gone on a business trip and will be home soon. My heart is like a lead weight in my chest. I've resorted to taking sleeping pills because I can't sleep. I lie awake and stare at the ceiling, then I toss and turn. I'm so depressed. I just feel heavy. Tears well up when I talk about him. I see him lying in his hospital bed, intubated, eyes closed. Trying to get that image out of my head, I look at pictures of him when he was healthy. I can't believe I'm a widow going to a grief support group. It's just not real. I'm too young to be a widow and he was too healthy to die. I just can't believe it.

How do I handle this? I don't want this journey. I want my partner back. I want to hang out at Starbuck's with him, hold his hand when he's 70. I want us to watch the kids grow up. Now what? I have to make all the decisions myself. What about all our plans? Now I have to plan by myself.

Mickey, you were so scared in the last weeks of your life. Please let me know you are OK. Please send me a sign. I want you to be at peace. I hope I comforted you while you were sick. I did absolutely everything I could to help you and keep you comfortable. I'm sorry you were so sick and weak. I know you wouldn't have wanted to linger long being so ill and incapacitated. You declined so fast, we didn't really have time to cope with what was happening.

People tell me I'm strong. I don't know what that means. I don't feel strong. I know I have to make decisions, so I do; but I don't really care about them. I just do them to get them done. I will work at getting through this grief so that I can function, but I know I'll never find another you. You were the love of my life. I think about you constantly. Be my angel and be with me and help me through this.

3
BLIND DATE

Kansas City

Oddly enough, one of the most influential people in our lives turned out to be a casual, mutual acquaintance that Mickey and I shared. Neither of us knew Beth very well. She and I worked out at the same gym and occasionally chatted. Mickey's kids worked with her in a restaurant that she managed; Craig was a bartender and Meredith a hostess. One day Mickey visited the restaurant, struck up a conversation with Beth, and mentioned that he missed being in a romantic relationship. He confessed that would really like to meet someone. I have no idea why I popped into her head, but I'm glad that I did.

As we hit our stride on treadmills the next time we met at the gym, Beth stated nonchalantly, "I have someone I'd like to introduce you to. Are you interested?" I was caught off guard a bit. It wasn't a discussion I had expected to have that morning. I hesitated for a moment as the thought flashed through my brain: *do you want to go on a blind date?* I had never been on one and didn't relish the idea of going on a date with someone I had never seen before. "Possibly," I replied. "First of all, is he attractive, and secondly, does he dress nicely?" In hindsight, I considered those such shallow questions, but I had been on some awful dates in recent months and was so tired of guys that were rude, angry, self-centered, and constantly talked about how much they hated their exs. She smiled and assured me that he was very nice looking and, because he was a clothing salesman, he was also a stylish dresser. That was enough to go on, so I gave her my number to pass on to him.

He called soon after—right in the middle of a neighborhood holiday party that I was hosting. I asked him to call back in a couple of hours, secretly pleased that I had been busy and didn't come across as too anxious to speak.

At 10:30 pm the phone rang, and a pleasant voice responded to my hello. "Hi Rose, my name is Mickey Weintraub. How are you?"

We fell into a conversation with ease, chatting about basic aspects of our lives. I told him that I owned my own home, had a successful nursing career, no children, had been married once before, and had lived in Kansas City for about five years. He filled me in about his two children, their ages, interests, and aspirations. I was so pleased to hear Mickey talk glowingly of Meredith and Craig, and that he didn't blast his ex-wife like so many of my dates had done. I had grown weary of others demonizing their fomer wives and lamenting about their kids on drugs.

We talked for quite a while before he asked if I would like to go out to dinner with him. I agreed. "Great, I'll pick you up around 6:30 on Saturday," he said enthusiastically. I balked at the suggestion; living alone had made me cautious. I usually didn't let guys pick me up on the first date at my home. I proposed to meet him at the restaurant, but he wouldn't hear of it. My mind raced, imagining different scenarios. Beth wouldn't set me up with a jerk, I wondered? I didn't know her well, but well enough that I could tell that she was a nice person and wouldn't hook me up with a weirdo. So, I eventually relented.

Although I had no expectations that our night out would be spectacular, I couldn't help but hope that Mickey was as nice as he sounded on the phone. Saturday rolled around and, as a car pulled into my driveway, I was surprised to feel butterflies in my stomach. The bell rang and I opened the door to an attractive, smiling face. "Hi Rose, I'm Mickey."

Hmmm, I thought—not bad, not bad at all.

He was tall, dressed impeccably and had such an engaging way about him. He helped me into my coat, and as he opened the car door for me, he said, "I hope you like Chinese?"

"I love it," I replied.

And off we went to the restaurant. So far, so good.

As we entered the Princess Garden, the owner greeted us with, "Hiya Mickey. How are you?"

"I'm great Wendy; this is Rose."

I have to say, I was impressed that the owner knew him by name. Then as she walked us to our table, we received a slew of warm welcomes from other customers, bussers, and wait staff. "Hi, Mickey." "How's it going, Mickey?" "Looking good Mickey."

Wow, did this guy know everyone in town?"

We sat down at our table and looked at the menu.

"Everything sounds so good!" I said.

"Everything is great!" Mickey replied.

We ordered and started talking.

"I suppose you like sports?" I asked.

"Yes, I love sports. My son was a top-ranked tennis player in his teen years. Unfortunately, he got burned out and quit, but we still play tennis together. I love all sports: tennis; basketball; football; baseball—love it all. How about you—what are your interests?"

"I love going to the gym, running, reading, cooking. Sports are OK with me; don't mind watching them on TV."

"What about your family?"

We had a wonderful meal and thoroughly enjoyed our time together. We talked about everything from our families to where we've lived, what we liked to ear, to movies. He told me about his marriage and divorce and I told him about my marriage and divorce. We both tried to make our marriages work, but they ended anyway. We had a lot in common. Although there was a comfort between us, I still felt somewhat guarded since I had been disappointed so many times. When Mickey revealed that he was eight years older than I was, my first reaction was that he was too old. But as I observed him, I thought, he seemed much younger. He was fit and had a youthful energy about him. He clicked enough boxes for me, so I figured that I needed to see how things would play out.

On the drive home, I was flooded with a host of silly, wonderful, teenage questions. *Will he walk me to the door? Should I invite him in? Will he ask me out again? What if he tries to kiss me? What will I do?* To say that Mickey was the perfect gentleman would be an understatement. He opened my car door and walked me just inside my house. He looked sincerely into my eyes and said, "I had a really nice time, Rose. Is it okay if we do this again?" Then he asked if he could kiss me. He pressed his lips gently onto mine for just a moment.

My heart lurched.

Mickey left and as I shut the door I instantly thought, "Oh yeah, there's something to this after all." I had no idea what joys were in store.

4
THE ART OF THE DANCE

Kansas City

As it turned out, my second date with Mickey was only two days after the first! It was early December, just a week or two before Christmas when he called to ask if I wanted to see the Nutcracker with him at the Kansas City Ballet. "Of course, I would," I said without hesitation. Normally, I wouldn't have agreed to see him again so quickly, but two things played a part: I took pleasure in his company, and Tchaikovsky's classic was an absolute favorite of mine.

The last-minute notice was because he had planned on taking his daughter to the event, but she had gotten ill. I thought it was so sweet that he wanted to share that with her. Nonetheless, I was thrilled to be attending the Sunday matinee in Meredith's place.

The theatre buzzed with activity as we waited for the performance to begin. Mickey leaned toward me, beaming with boyish spontaneity, and announced how much he loved ballet.

"Really?" I said incredulously. "You love ballet?"

I assumed that he had bought the tickets only to please his daughter, never thinking that he actually took pleasure in it. Most guys I knew were bored to death at the mere mention of ballet and, if forced to go, would doze through the whole show. But Mickey regarded it as a very athletic art form. In particular, he loved to watch Mikhail Baryshnikov dance. He was so impressed with his muscular physique, strength, and agility – how he could leap through the air and suspend himself for so long. He also had great respect for Baryshnikov's courage to defect from Russia and move to the United States to live out his dreams. That night, we were both captivated by the performance of the Nutcracker. I snuck glances in Mickey's direction enjoying his reactions as the tempo of the dances shifted. Every now and then, I felt him peeking at me too. In particular, the passionate, swelling music of the Pas de Deux seemed to create a tenderness between us. It was such a lovely way for us to get to know each other better, without exchanging a word.

And so, our dance had begun... .

On the drive home afterward, Mickey talked enthusiastically about the company's upcoming schedule and asked if I would like to join him for another production in the near future.

"I would love it!" I said.

In a reasonably short time, we had discovered two common interests – Chinese food and ballet. There would be many more to come.

As it happened, after the third or fourth ballet we attended, every time the lights went down and the show began, I noticed Mickey starting to doze off. I thought it was so funny–guess he had been on best behavior the first few times. The exception was when Baryshnikov came to town to perform with his "White Oak Project." Mickey was absolutely mesmerized by Mikhail; he just couldn't believe how beautifully he danced.

So, of course, one of our Christmas traditions became watching Baryshnikov dance in his 1977 televised version of the Nutcracker. We viewed it every year without fail.

To this day, I watch it at least once during every Christmas season. The memory of how much Mickey loved it still makes me cry.

Journal Entry
JANUARY 19, 2008

My Love—

    I spoke with Melby today—your fellow clothing rep who you knew so well and became such good friends with. We talked a long time about you. He wanted to know what happened and why you got so sick so fast. At the end of the conversation, he said he was so sorry for my loss. I told him I was also sorry for his loss because he lost a good friend. That made him very sad, and he started to cry. You made such an impact on people's lives. We talked about how you always called Kim (Melby's wife) at 7:15 a.m. just to talk. You'd say "Top of the morning to you, darlin'" and how I'd always tell you it was too early to call. You didn't care and Kim liked it and knew she'd be delayed about 20 minutes. You really didn't know her very well, but you had such an easy way talking to people that they didn't mind just chatting. You had a lot of good friends who cared about you so much. They always say they take part of you with them. Things you said or things you did. That is really a huge compliment to you.

    I continue to feel alone. I now have to make meals for one and that's not easy. Little things trigger the realization that you're not here. I still look at your picture all the time. My sweet man is gone from my life. I look for you all the time. Come to me anytime.

    I love you.

5

BEFORE MICKEY

I grew up in a large, boisterous, Catholic family that had an unwavering belief in God. We went to church every Sunday and confession every other Saturday, to affirm our faith. When I was in grade school, I sang in the church choir and often attended Mass during the week as well. We prayed the rosary and observed all church holy days. We participated in many religious functions–dinners, games, dances, meetings. The church was our driving force. The church was our anchor.

Yet, when I entered my adolescence, many questions floated through my mind and the anchor began to slowly unmoor. All at once, I had become cognizant of the world around me—outside of the church. The thought of spending so much time in its clutches no longer appealed to me and I weighed the sincerity of my devotion. But the doctrine was so ingrained in me that I couldn't even consider skipping Sunday Mass until I was well out of highschool.

The possibility of getting caught the first time that I did skip out was such an adrenaline rush. I thought for sure that my sin would be discovered, but it wasn't. That emboldened me to do it a second time and a third and a fourth. By the time I reached my twenties, I was rarely seen sharing a pew amongst the pious congregants.

I got married when I was 25, then divorced when I was 32—the first person to do so in my family. At first, I thought that I was in love with my husband, but after a few years, I accepted that the marriage wasn't working. I had already become a head nurse and he was still trying to figure out what he wanted to do in life. We tried to make a go of it, and I supported him in any way that I could, but eventually, he became depressed and under the grip of other destructive behavior: drinking and drugs. Since I was hoping to raise children, I wanted a partner that I could rely on. The marriage fell apart and divorce was inevitable.

Even though my family agreed that it was the right thing to do, I felt a tremendous sense of guilt that I had let them down. Having been the middle child of seven in my family, I sometimes had gotten lost in the shuffle. That, and the fact that my father often wasn't around, may have contributed to a lack of self-confidence. Overall, I had a wonderful childhood, but I sometimes hesitated to act on my convictions. To this day, I don't know what possessed me, but I called my parish priest and requested an annulment. I suppose I thought I could save face with an annulment as opposed to a divorce. Nonetheless, for me, it was a gutsy thing to do.

The priest was perfunctory. He set the process in motion with an interview, followed by a ridiculous amount of paperwork that was then sent to the bishop for review. The hoops that the Catholic Church asked me to jump through infuriated me. My appeal seemed insignificant compared to other issues, such as child abuse, subjugation of women, and dictatorial leadership. Eventually, the annulment was granted, and I found myself freefalling. Despite my misgivings about the church, I longed to have the security of an anchor once more and thought maybe religion would offer me something that I was lacking. So, I became an avid church-goer again.

When I first met Mickey, I was attending Mass every Sunday with a friend of mine. Even though Mickey was Jewish, it was of no consequence to him. Likewise, he would go to synagogue on the High Holy Days. Our differing religions had no effect on either of us. By the time I realized that our relationship was becoming serious, an exceptional parish priest had taken over the helm at my church. He was down to earth and realistic and gave such inspiring sermons. Still, I was a bit apprehensive when I approached him about marrying Mickey. I was unclear about the rules for marrying outside of my religion. But in his friendly manner, he essentially said, "Your faith is strong, go get married, and stop with the guilt." It was a welcome response.

There was such a distinct contrast in how I felt when I met Mickey compared to my first marriage. It was clear to me that I had found my life partner. He was considerate, kind, and supportive. I was certain that together, we could deal with anything thrown our way.

6
COUNTRY CLUB

Kansas City, Taos

We were married at an elegant country club eighteen months after we first met. We sent out seventy-five invitations with the expectation that maybe sixty people would show. We were wrong. To our pleasant surprise, seventy-five chairs were set up and every one of them was filled.

As the big day approached, we had a lot of fun searching for our wedding outfits. Mickey selected a handome, grey suit with a beautiful matching tie, colored with reds. I found an off-white, satin, tea-length dress with a lacy back that ended in a large bow just below my waist. White heels with sheer white hose completed the ensemble.

My four lovely bridesmaids were: Mickey's daughter, Meredith, who was nineteen, and three of my nieces. Melissa was ten, Sarah, seven, and Emily, six. Sarah and I had a special bond because we were both left-handed and we both loved the color pink. So, I knew the color would play an integral role when I got married. All the girls were thrilled about being asked to be in the wedding and that their dresses would be pink.

Emily, my youngest sister's daughter, being only six years old, was a little concerned about what she had to do at the wedding. I told her that we were getting married at a country club and that all she had to do was walk down the aisle. The only country club she was familiar with was the name of a grocery store where she lived in Minnesota. She couldn't understand why we were getting married at a grocery store, but she was confident that she could walk down the aisle, as she did it all the time with her mother.

As it turned out, Emily's family provided a few moments of comedy to the day. After the ceremony, I found out that her father had forgotten to bring dress pants for the wedding. Being the "creative" person he was—and by that, I mean cheap—he went to K-mart and bought a pair of slacks, hemmed them with scotch tape, only to return them after the wedding. In addition, Emily's older brother retreated to his hotel room during the reception and previewed twenty-five videos in just over ten minutes and they got charged for all twenty-five movies! However, my sister and brother-in-law talked to the hotel manager, explained the situation, and the costs were reversed.

The music swelled and we all lined up. Mickey and his best man, his twenty-one-year-old son, Craig, walked down the aisle first and turned toward the audience. Next came Meredith, then Melissa, both gorgeous and glowing. But there was a collective, "Awww..." when the two cutest girls in the room followed, holding each other's hand, and clutching their flower baskets in the other. As I strolled down the aisle embraced by my parents on either side of me, a friend softly played the piano. My heart fluttered as I glimpsed up and saw my Mickey smiling. I joyfully walked toward my love, my companion, my soulmate.

We stood together in front of all our witnesses and spoke the sweet vows we had written for each other. We took a sip of wine from a glass that we had made especially for the occasion, with our names and the date engraved on it. We listened to the minister speak a few encouraging words. The ceremony was short and sweet, probably only fifteen minutes long. Still, Sarah and Emily were a little restless and wiggled and turned every which way. Melissa mouthed "stand still" and Sarah stuck her tongue out at her. Sarah got a stern glance from me and she looked so guilty that I couldn't help but smile. At the end of the service, Mickey followed the Jewish tradition of smashing a glass with his foot. Actually, it was a light bulb wrapped in a napkin as it was a little too dangerous to smash a real glass. A few people shouted, "Mazel tov" and we were married. The wedding had gone off without a hitch.

We walked into the reception area after everyone had said their congratulations on the receiving line and were greeted by an exuberant round of applause. It was fantastic to have both of our families and our close friends gathered for the first time. While people helped themselves to the buffet and open bar, we made sure that we talked to every one of them. Several hours passed as we were showered with well wishes, immersed in old stories, and got caught up in the positive feeling that permeated the room. I was so happy that I didn't want the day to end.

We were scheduled to leave that night for our honeymoon in Taos to stay at a friend's hacienda. On the way home, Mickey revealed to me that the key hadn't arrived. It was supposed to have come earlier in the week. Mickey called Charlie two weeks earlier and he said he had mailed the key. We were so busy with the wedding we just assumed the key would arrive on time. As soon as we walked in the door, Mickey got on the phone in an attempt to contact Charlie. Mickey called everyone he could think of but couldn't find him. "We can't fly to New Mexico; we don't even know where the hacienda is," I said with urgency. "What are we going to do? We can't get on the plane without a place to stay."

Mickey was getting very worried and stressed. His plan for a beautiful honeymoon in the Southwest was rapidly falling apart.

Finally, after a few nerve-wracking hours, Charlie called back. "Where's the key,? We never got it!" Mickey said in a panicked voice. "Our flight leaves in a couple of hours and we have no idea what to do." After a few minutes of back and forth, a plan was arranged to get the key from a shop owner in Taos. It turned out that Charlie had sent it to the wrong address.

At last, we were off to the airport. I carried my bouquet with me as we got on the check-in line. The woman at the counter asked if we were newlyweds. "Yes, we are," we beamed.

"I think I can do something special for you," she said flashing a big smile. She proceeded to upgrade us to first class.

Similarly, as we were waiting in line to board the plane, we started chatting with a flight attendant. He also asked us if we had just gotten married. Neither of us had flown first class before and were so excited to slip into our luxurious seats as the rest of the passengers boarded. We enjoyed a smooth, comfortable flight, eager to reach our destination. As we began our descent into Albuquerque, the same flight attendant came over and gave us a bottle of red wine. "Have a great life together," he said warmly. And with that, he turned and was gone. We looked at each other in disbelief. "What a kind gesture," Mickey said with glee.

We landed, got our rental car, checked the map, and started our climb to Taos. The rolling mountains, the desert terrain, and the winding road made a strong impression on us. As we entered Taos, we were struck by the size of it; it was much smaller than we had anticipated. We followed the instructions to the shop that Charlie had given us, to get the key, relieved to find the proprietor there. She pointed us in the general direction of the hacienda and we were on our way.

Everything looked the same to us: old; rundown; dirt roads; and lots of sheep and pigs. "Oh boy," I thought. "This is not what I expected. This is no country club." I could tell by the look on Mickey's face that it wasn't what he had hoped for either. After searching for a while, we finally found the alley where the hacienda was supposed to be located. However, we had trouble finding the door since there were no numbers on the dilapidated buildings.

"Why would Charlie send us here? He said it was a nice place," Mickey complained.

I put my hand on his shoulder. "Maybe this isn't the right area. I guess we can find a hotel if we need to. It'll be all right."

Our search eventually led us to a door that we guessed might be the right one. We sighed with relief as the key turned in the lock. The door creaked loudly as we gingerly pushed it open and peered in. The upside was that the hacienda had indeed been restored. But it was musty and filled with spider webs that clung to our faces as we walked through.

Mickey was visibly concerned and disappointed. I took his hand and said, "Let's just open the windows and get some fresh air in here and we'll knock down some of the cobwebs. If it's still awful, we'll find somewhere else to stay tomorrow. We'll figure it out. Don't worry."

Mickey looked at me and said, "I'm sorry about this. I wanted it to be so special."

"It'll be okay, don't worry," I reassured.

I walked into the kitchen to open the window. "Whoa," I said and held my nose. The window looked out over a muddy pig pen, featuring a huge sow lounging in the slush. Mickey rushed over and with a straight face said, "Well, there's tomorrow's breakfast."

We both burst out laughing—something we sorely needed. Maybe it wouldn't be so bad after all.

It was April in Taos and although sunny, we were at a high elevation, so it was cold. We looked around for a thermostat to turn up the heat, but of course, there wasn't one. However, we had a stack of wood and two kiva fireplaces—tall, thin structures built in the pueblo tradition. The challenge was: how did two city slickers build a fire in a kiva? Things just kept getting better...

Luckily, I remembered reading somewhere that you should stack wood vertically in a kiva. We built up the fire until a strong heat filled the room. As we laid on the bed and watched the flames dancing, it felt kind of romantic – at least for a while. Subsequently, the fire died down and it was cold again. I had brought a pretty negligee for our first night as a married couple, but I couldn't even think about wearing it. Instead, we rummaged through drawers and found sweaters, wool socks, and flannel shirts to put on. Although we piled blankets on top of us, we still woke several times during the night, freezing. We could see our breath. I don't think I've ever been so cold.

It certainly wasn't the beginning of the honeymoon we had dreamed of.

With some trepidation, we wondered what lay ahead.

7
HONEYMOON

Taos

Although our marriage had a rocky introduction, our time in Taos evolved into a rather gratifying adventure. When Mickey and I arose early on the first morning, we decided to go in search of food and discovered that, in essence, we were staying in a sleepy, small town. We were unable to find a single restaurant that was open at 9 a.m. After walking around for a while, we finally came across someone who told us about a place that provided breakfast. It turned out to be well worth the wait. It was a cute, cozy café that served a variety of delicious, savory, and sweet Mexican dishes that we washed down with strong, tasty coffee. It was a great beginning to our day.

Taos finally came alive at 11 am when the stores began to open their doors. We really chuckled when we read a sign posted at one establishment that read, "Open 10ish, Close 5ish." We were there at 10:30 and there was still no sign of life. As we strolled around town, we visited several charming boutiques and a few lovely art galleries. We found the shop owners to be incredibly friendly and had a blast asking them questions about their village and joking with them.

One of our main goals in Taos was to explore the R.C. Gorman Navajo Gallery. Both Mickey and I were big fans of his art. R.C., who first came to Taos in 1964, was a native of Arizona, raised in the Navajo tradition, and established his gallery in 1968.

Since that time, he had attained worldwide recognition and fame, as well as a reputation as a real character about town. In fact, he was an iconic staple of Taos culture. We eagerly climbed a hill toward his gallery and gasped with delight when we entered. It was our dream come true to be surrounded by his beautiful, vibrant paintings of round, native women.

Eventually, we started a conversation with the saleswoman in the gallery and, of course, Mickey mentioned that if R.C. just happened to be there, we would really like to meet him. Without hesitating, she said, "Actually, he's across the street having lunch. Don't tell anyone I told you. He loves talking to people, so go on over."

We couldn't believe our luck. As soon as we went through the restaurant door, we spotted him sitting at a table in the back. We were so excited to be escorted to a table near him. When the waiter came over, we asked if he would mind asking R.C. if we could speak with him for a minute. The waiter smiled. "Sure, go over and say hi; he doesn't mind."

But we insisted that he ask permission first. He approached R.C., whispered to him, and the artist motioned for us to come over.

Mickey said:

"Hello, Mr. Gorman. We are huge fans of your work. We are so excited to meet you. We came all the way from Kansas City to meet you."

"Well, thank you. I'm so glad you like my work. How do you like Taos? Have you ever been here before?"

We sat and talked with him a bit and had the best time. We couldn't believe how friendly and gracious he was. He even posed for photos with us and signed one of his books that we had purchased. We were absolutely thrilled. We thanked him again and said we didn't want to disturb his lunch. We were so excited as we walked back to our table. We couldn't take our eyes off the artist.

For many reasons that experience will always be dear to my heart. It really made our honeymoon memorable and eclipsed any misgivings that we might have had at the start.

8
DARKNESS CREEPING

Sedona 2008

I'd been set out to sea in a flimsy boat with no paddle and no rudder.

Strong winds took me in all directions. The waters churned and the waves were rough. I couldn't get my bearings. I was off course. I was afloat.

I'd returned to our home in Sedona. I waited for the phone call that never arrived. Was he on a business trip? When would he be home? Lying awake at night—eyes wide open—no sleep would come. I resorted to taking sleeping pills so my mind would quiet and I could get some rest; sometimes it worked, sometimes not.

There was a lead weight in my chest, yet I felt like I had no substance, like a paper doll cut out of a magazine. I felt hollow— no bones, no muscle, no brain. I couldn't think straight, couldn't get control of my emotions, couldn't make a decision. What had happened to me? Maybe I needed to just go where he was—but where was that? It wouldn't take much to let go. Who cared? Assuredly, not me.

Within six months I had lost the two most important people in my heart—my mother, who was the sweetest, kindest, most loving person, raised seven children and was on this earth for 92 years, and my dear husband, Mickey. My life was so depressing and I didn't want to be here anymore. My thoughts prowled around my mind like a panther creeping in, ready to spring forth, throw me to the ground and gnaw at me. I'd never contemplated suicide, until then. It would be easy for me. Fear gripped me once again and I lost control. I was drowning. I was a shipwreck, slipping under the surface to be submerged forever.

I thought about Mickey all the time., but I couldn't bring myself to talk about him; tears welled up, and my voice cracked. I tried to dwell on positive memories and how much we loved each other. He was so attractive, always holding my hand or putting his arm around me. Out of the millions of people in the world, he'd picked me.

He had such a sweetness about him.

"How about I take my best gal out to dinner?" he'd say when I returned home from work. I loved that. I loved our favorite song, "Here and Now" by Luther Vandross. I loved how he made me feel so special.

As I sat alone in the dark, my heart was shrouded in disbelief. Nothing seemed real. I was too young to be a widow and Mickey had been too young to die. I'd never been a depressed person and always tried to find good in everything—but now? How could I handle this? I didn't want to be in a universe that had shifted so drastically.

Decisions? He was not here to talk them over; they were mine alone to make. Goals? We had set them every day; now my days were empty. Plans? We had a blueprint for our future, a future that never would be realized.

I felt panicked most of the time. Panic ended at death, so maybe I needed to join him in the afterlife… or wherever you go. We would be together, and I would be happy. I missed the laughs, the inside jokes and the knowing nods meant only for each other. I wanted my partner back.

How could I reset my compass? How could I get a grip? How

could I start this life journey all over again? I was so weary. Maybe I wouldn't start over, maybe I should just end it.

9
VOODOO

Sedona 2008

Thoughts of suicide hovered like a bee waiting to land, stinging me with hopelessness and raising welts.

Day upon day of feeling lost had become monotonous and boring. Sitting in my chair, staring out the window at nothing, intermittent crying, had become all too routine. My purpose eluded me. I was no longer actively living. Get up—alone, walk the dog—alone, get ready for work, go to work, come home from work, walk the dog—alone, eat dinner—alone, watch TV or read—alone, go to bed—alone. I was keenly aware that I was flying solo. Just me.

Although family and friends would visit now and then, I couldn't tolerate the charade. "How are you doing Rose?"

"I'm okay" I'd say with tears brimming in my eyes.

My world was collapsing, but why bother telling them the truth; they couldn't possibly understand. They'd only give me that sad-eyed look that drove me crazy. Then they'd add a platitude like, "Oh, it'll be alright– you'll see." How should I possibly respond? I wanted to scream, yeah,

R I G H T! Thanks for that! But I just nodded my head: "Yes, I will be ok."

I had never thought much about death before. Sure, I expected my elderly parents to die, but losing my husband in his prime caused existential questions to flood my brain. *What is the purpose of life? Why do we die? Why did Mickey have to die? Where do you go when you die? Would anyone I knew have some insight?* I hesitated to contact family and friends, aware that they had their own lives to manage. They didn't need the extra burden of my searching, my sorrow.

But there came a time when my inner turmoil reached such a height that I decided if I were to survive, it was vital to be amongst the living. I began to meet friends frequently for coffee. Most of the women were very caring and intuitive and could see how I struggled with my thoughts. Many of them had spiritual inclinations, something that I had not explored since I considered it to be flaky.

One day I was sitting with my friends, Brenda and James, who are both psychologists and married to one another. Brenda was ever the optimist but wasn't someone who over-analyzed or tried to fix people. She listened attentively to my inquiries and heartaches. She knew I had gone to a grief support group for six weeks. I could have gone on to the next group, but I didn't want to continue. I could have gone to a grief counselor, but just didn't want to do that either. Her concern was apparent. As I raised my coffee cup to take a big gulp, she said, "Why don't you have an astrology reading?"

I just about choked. As I put my cup down, she must have read the shock crossing my face. "What? Why? How would that help?" I stammered.

"It might answer some questions and bring you some peace. Think about it," she softly replied.

No way; how can that "voodoo" stuff answer my questions? I don't believe in any of that nonsense and I don't intend to spend my hard-earned money on a "reading."

Brenda sensed my skepticism and gently suggested, "Rose, you are searching for answers. This might help– it's worth a try."

My frenzied brain tossed the idea around for a while as one side said, "Go on, give it a whirl," and the other side said, "It's a waste of time and money." It was a struggle. Part of me wanted to crawl into a hole and die and another part of me knew that I couldn't. I had responsibilities. Family members, pets, and people at work depended on me. What if I did do the reading? I didn't need to tell anyone about it. People had enough to handle with their own issues and didn't need to become embroiled in my conflict.

Experts warn about making bad decisions after experiencing a trauma. I certainly didn't want to go down the wrong path, but I didn't know what else to do. It was clear that I had to do something. I've never been a gambler, but I trusted my friend and knew that she would never recommend a charlatan. Brenda gave me the astrologist's name and number.

Several days went by and I still hadn't made the phone call. After further deliberation, I finally took the plunge and looked at Robert's website to research his education and training. He was a Vedic astrologer—whatever that was. The content on his website was informative and put me somewhat at ease. I continued to be plagued with doubts, but I also felt intrigued. I wasn't clear what pushed me—maybe Mickey's spirit—but I begrudgingly typed in my credit card number and email address to schedule the reading. It was to be done over the phone from Robert's home in Oregon to mine in Arizona. How this was possible—I hadn't a clue.

Throughout the next few days, I checked my emails often, curious as to when the momentous event would take place. I was committed now. But the more time passed, the less secure I became. He had requested some basic information such as where and when I was born but nothing more. Receipt of a confirmation email alleviated my stress and, finally, the day came.

My heart pounded as I reached for the phone. My hand shook as I pulled it away, then tried again, and finally dialed his number. My expectations were low. I was sure that he would be some type of weirdo.

His soothing voice came on the line. "Hello, this is Robert." He sounded like a normal person.

"Hi Robert, this is Rose."

We chatted for a few minutes about his background, where he lived and Vedic astrology.

The pounding in my chest subsided as he gently referred to my astrological chart, which he had asked me to print out in advance. I had never seen anything like it. The chart looked like gibberish to me. There were planets listed with time spans of beginning and ending dates, and graphs with different "houses" and "planets" in them. I was fascinated with the extensive information Robert was able to ascertain from this chart. He went through several groups of years and was able to pinpoint exact things that had happened to me. It gave me goose bumps. How could he possibly know?

His reading from a planetary chart told of things that had happened in the recent past. For instance, the 1990's were a "hard work" period for me—and he was right! I had an extremely important management job and simultaneously went back to school for an advanced degree. Robert also told me that the "Rahu" period is one of disruptions and transitions. My Rahu period was from July 2006 to May 2009. During that period my Mother died (June 2007), Mickey died (December 2007) and I moved from Sedona back to Kansas City (2008). I would agree that that was a period of disruptions and transitions.

I hadn't told him anything before the reading and I was so surprised with how much he was able to intuit about me. I was slowly becoming a believer.

The original impetus to agree to a reading was to find out why my husband had died. I had little faith that Robert could impart such knowledge, but I craved some understanding about it—anything. The other reason was that I was incredibly scared about my future. I didn't know what lay ahead and I wanted reassurance that I would be okay—probably a natural reaction after a trauma. I was fishing in the middle of an ocean with a whale caught in my line.

Prior to the reading, I only had told Robert that my husband had died. I longed to know why he'd passed so young and so quickly. I gave him Mickey's birth date, where he was born and the approximate time of his birth. I was stunned with the results. Apparently, Mickey had a problematic alignment of planets surrounding him when he was born, and Robert could see that his time on earth would be short-lived. He also saw cancer and infection in Mickey's chart without knowing that, in fact, Mickey had died of a massive infection from the cancer. I was overcome with emotion by this improbable message, but a warm glow filled my heart.

The reading that I had railed against had turned out to be one of the most profound experiences of my life. As it happened, I would return many times for many years to enjoy what Robert had to tell me. Astrology became a wonderfully important part of my life. No longer dismissive of it, I believe whole heartedly in his readings.

My limited view of the world had broken open. I started to think that perhaps there was something to this new-age approach to living. Initially fearing that I was going to be taken advantage of by con artists and fakes, I experienced a complete turnaround. I was now convinced that astrology was a credible field and I wanted to learn more. My thirst for knowledge had accelerated.

Days passed. I sat in my chair gazing out the window, drinking my coffee as usual, but I felt like I had changed. I began to actively seek out "alternative" ideas. I had never meditated before, but as I read about it, I wanted to try it. I wanted to find the peace people spoke about, emptying my head of the old thoughts that swirled around, that kept me from sleeping, that invaded my mind, and nibbled at my attention. I read books and listened to tapes on how to meditate and began to do so. It was difficult at first. I couldn't keep my mind from wandering. What would I do at work tomorrow, what plans would I make for the weekend, what groceries did I need to get? When my grocery list appeared, I realized I was completely off track. I simply opened my eyes, settled in, and started over. Sitting at the head of my bed with myback against the wall, I would take a couple of deep breaths and repeat a straightforward mantra: RELAX. When my mind started drifting, I would bring it back to RELAX. I found some calming music that helped to keep my mind focused. Little by little, I found my way.

Meditation became my lifeline to peace. I felt more at ease and in control of my thoughts to a greater degree. If I had rushed around during the day, I could put my mind to rest and transmute the pressure. So, I started meditating every night before I went to sleep. Turning off the light in the bedroom, I would light a candle, settle into a cross-legged sitting position at the top of my bed and set my intention. As I progressed, I was open to whatever came my way, anything I could learn. It slowed me down, quieted my mind and decreased my heart rate.

Eventually, to my amazement, I found myself drifting into other realms. One evening I was deep into meditation and I visualized ancient Egypt. As Robert had once described, it was there that I had lived as a high priestess. In this instance, I could clearly see that I was conducting a funeral for a person of royalty. A parade of dark-skinned people adorned in sparkling robes of gold, blue, and red, moved about in their strappy sandals, laced up to their knees. Many wore golden turbans.

The deceased was carried in a large, ornate coffin on poles placed on the shoulders of several young men. A long procession wound slowly through the interior of the pyramid. I could smell the damp, earthy scent of the floor and the oily smell of the torches that lit the way. Everyone was cast in a brilliant glow, reflected from the torches. It was evident that the deceased was an important person and the responsibility of carrying out my task weighed upon me. I lit incense and uttered ritualistic prayers. The coffin was set down and the pallbearers filed out of the pyramid. Several in attendance set gifts next to the deceased that he would take to the other world. And, then, for a reason unknown to me, my eyes popped open and the meditation was over. I don't think I had ever gone so deep.

The changes that I went through were monumental. This "stuff" that I had so long considered crazy was actually transformational, awe-inspiring, and real. I could have chosen a different route. I could have become a religious fanatic or become an alcoholic or an addict. I could have found all kinds of negative behaviors to keep me from being me. But I didn't. Ever so slowly, I started to crawl out of the soul-robbing hole that I'd inhabited for months and, for the first time in a long time, I felt hope. Miraculously, people started showing up in my life that would help me find my way.

Journal entry
JANUARY 22, 2008

You should see the moon, Mickey. It's full and bright. I saw it setting this a.m. on my way to work, slowly creeping down toward the red rocks. Then on my way home, it was rising, and again, was full and bright, rising up from the red rocks. It's the same moon that shines on you and that gives me comfort. We both see the same moon. Oh, how I miss you.. Who can I enjoy the night sky with? Who can I tell things to? I want to share things with you throughout the day and I write to you, but don't get a response. I miss your stories, your humor.

I got a letter from the Mathis's today. Their kids are 16, 14, and 12. Can you believe it? They look so grown up. They used to be our "pseudo-grandkids," before we had any. We watched those kids grow up from little toddlers. They had such nice things to say about you— and us. You made a memorable impact on people, babe. And you will live on in people. They will carry with them your good qualities. When I think of you, I try to do what you would do, in certain circumstances. I am picking up the phone more often and connecting with people instead of using email. You would have called people, so I try to do that now too. I'm trying to keep in contact with our couple friends—don't want to lose those connections.

So, I went to my grief support group tonight. I'm anxious to start the next session. It will help me feel more connected to the people in there. I feel so disconnected and like I'm in some other world.

I'm trying to keep going without you. I know you'd want me to go on. I honor your memory by continuing on.

I think of you constantly.

I love you.

10
MEETING NANCY

Minnesota 2008

Carol, the oldest of my four sisters, made her home in Rochester, Minnesota where the Mayo Clinic is located. It was wonderfully convenient to stay with her and her husband while Mickey underwent treatment. We appreciated the comforts of their large, beautiful home and the support of family.

They are empty nesters, apart from one "elderly child", their dear Springer Spaniel, Pepper. The bombardment of chemo and radiation that Mickey endured, left him incapable of anything but lying in bed or sitting in an easy chair. But wherever he was, Pepper was beside him. Mickey was so weak he never said a word to Pepper, never pet her, and most likely was unaware of her presence. We were stunned that Pepper had taken it upon herself to be his constant companion. While I had always known that this is a comon ability for dogs to sense when a person is ill, I'd never witnessed this phenomenon. It was nice to think that Pepper had brought some solace to Mickey when we were at a loss as to what to do.

A few months after Mickey's funeral, I returned to Carol's. I longed for the company of one of my sisters, a mainstay to keep me from slipping back into fear, despair, and depression. One day, Carol spoke to me about an interesting woman named Nancy whom she had recently befriended. They had met through an organization called SCORE, which was comprised of retired businesspeople who volunteered to mentor others who were seeking to build a business and to give financial advice. Carol was a volunteer. Nancy had approached the group with caution because the nature of her business was not conventional. She had a spiritual consulting company and she feared that she wouldn't be taken seriously. In addition, she was a lesbian and she and her long-time partner and son had encountered many biases over the years. After most of the group hesitated to take Nancy on, my sister jumped at the chance.

Nancy is a psychic who uses spirit guides, singing bowls, drums, and calls on the ancestors for advice. To understand the nature of Nancy's business, Carol had a couple of sessions with her. She was pleasantly surprised with how much she gained from the experience. During my visit, she encouraged me to book an appointment with Nancy. Not only was she a psychic but also a minister who held a Ph.D. in Counseling. Quite a unique combination of skills; I thought, why not? Seeing a counselor had not been a priority since Mickey's death and I figured maybe it was time to talk to a professional. As far as being a psychic and minister, I didn't give it much consideration – it wasn't important to me. She had a Ph.D., so I concluded that she probably had something to offer.

Carol made an appointment and drove me to Nancy's with the assurance that she would return for me in an hour. As I climbed the steps to her office, I was greeted by the faint sound of Native American flute music. I have always loved the sound of those flutes; they are so peaceful and soothing to my ears. They resonate with me, as if calling up a long distant memory. When I arrived at her office door, it was open. "Rose, welcome," she said warmly. I don't know why, but I immediately felt a connection to her, like I had known her for a long time.

As I sat on one of two cushiony sofas, I took in the ambiance of the room. A few candles flickered, accentuating the friendly

Southwestern décor. I noticed a dream catcher on the wall along with feathers and arrows. But, amongst the artifacts, my attention was drawn to two photographs. When I asked Nancy about them, she identified one as her mother and the other as her grandmother, both influential people in her life. From the time she was a child, Nancy had been acutely aware of her special gifts. But having grown up in a religious family, her mother forbade her to talk about them. It was her grandmother who had emboldened Nancy to develop her abilities. She acknowledged that she was also psychic and "saw" many things. She inspired Nancy to accept her gifts and not be frightened of them.

As Nancy sat across from me, I observed three gold bowls that looked like mortars with pestles placed on the coffee table. But as she took a mallet and struck one of the bowls, I realized that they had quite a unique function. A rich, deep tone filled the room with a soft vibration… and we began.

The only information that Carol had given Nancy was that my husband had recently died. As I talked a bit, she closed her eyes on and off. I wasn't sure what she was doing, but it seemed intentional. I decided to trust the process and relax into it. As we casually conversed, Nancy quietly announced that Mickey was here with me. She described him accurately as tall with dark hair and wearing a small hat. I was dumbfounded. *What? How is that possible? Why did she say that…was it some type of joke?* It made me so upset that I started to cry. I had wanted so desperately to have Mickey contact me and she nonchalantly revealed that he was with me? *Oh my God, what?* I didn't feel him, but she was so convinced that he was there.

"Mickey is here?"

"Yes, he is standing behind you with his hand on your shoulder.

He is smiling and saying he was so glad to be married to you. You gave him great comfort. He also is saying it is your life now and you should enjoy it. He is fine and he wants you to be happy."

I was crying now and trembling.

There were more disclosures to come. Apparently, I was also surrounded by many of my ancestors, telling me that I would be okay, that I was strong and would get through my situation. Incredibly, she gave a detailed description of both of my grandmothers. One of them, my maternal grandmother, was tall and thin with curly gray hair and wire-rimmed glasses. The other, my paternal grandmother, had white curly hair with darker wire-rimmed glasses and was shorter and rounder. One of my grandfathers also joined in.

Nancy looked far away as if she were seeing something in the distance. It was Mickey again, speaking about how good I was to him and how I did everything I could to make him better. It was just that he was destined to leave this world.

My emotions were so raw. At first, I thought that Nancy was being cruel, but I was stunned with the information that came through her. I didn't know how to respond, except to cry—not wailing sobs but big, full tears that wouldn't stop. The ache in my heart brought such a heaviness that I could barely breathe. It is not what I expected from my session.

It felt like I was starting to spin out of control again and I wondered why I was putting myself through so much pain. But I was desperate for answers to why Mickey had died and where my life was headed. As torturous as it was, if Nancy were able to shed some light on my situation, it would be helpful.

The hour was just about over—not that I had any presence of mind to keep track of time. All I knew was that I wanted to stay, and I wanted to keep Mickey there forever. I was whirling from what had taken place, astonished by all the people who had shown up. I was comforted by the messages I had received but also overwhelmed. As I continued to quiver and cry, Nancy picked up the mallet again and lightly struck the singing bowl. Both of us were startled at how loudly it rang. She said that it was due to the strong vibrations present from our time together.

Being fairly wrung out, I didn't ask what she meant by that, but simply thanked her for a fascinating time. She encouraged me to call her anytime and proposed some assignments to delve into, assignments that could be done long distance via the internet. This very much appealed to me since I wasn't working with a counselor. Anything that could assist me in moving on was a step in the right direction.

We gave each other a big hug; she could see that I was visibly shaken.

She said to me: *"Your life is like a big tapestry that has some threads pulled out. You need to weave the back of the tapestry together to make it whole again. You can do it, but it will take a lot of work. If you need me, just call me. I will do whatever I can to help you put the tapestry together again."*

"Thank you, Nancy."

Her arms wrapped around me like a big, fluffy blanket. A sense of familiarity passed between us and, in that moment, I knew that Nancy would play an important role in my growth.

11
BLOOD BOILS

Sedona 2008

Time is measured by how long it's been since Mickey passed. A few weeks went by, then a few months. I was caught in a stagnant loop of sadness.

I was frightened by an uncontrollable rage boiling up inside of me.

It had become nearly impossible to sustain the glimpses of well-being that I had acquired in my meetings with Robert and Nancy. Like a volcano ready to blow, I opened my mouth and hot lava, dirt, filth, and fire came spewing out. Perhaps I was possessed by a deranged monster that attacked at will. I didn't recognize myself in that angry, volatile person.

These feelings of rage started before I was regularly meditating. I didn't know how to control them. I would get so angry at situations and people. The rage would boil up and the words that came out of my mouth were hateful and foul. I tried so hard not to say them in front of people.

"Friends" started to dwindle away. I hadn't heard from my close neighbors, who used to check on me regularly. We'd often dine or walk our dogs together. No more.

I called my neighbors on the phone one morning: "Hi, guys—want to walk the dogs?"

"Uh, no we can't, we have errands to run…chores to do… other plans."

It was disappointing and hurtful. I was trying to get used to being alone and I needed the company of friends, but now they were drifting away. It made me incredibly sad.

Maybe Mickey's death had made them face their own mortality. Or maybe they didn't want to spend time with a person who couldn't get a grip on herself. But, I thought, that's what friends did for each other—stuck around, saw things through. Other neighbors from down the block had been taking my dog Zuni out for walks so I didn't have to worry about rushing home from work. But I returned home one day to see the message light blinking on my phone,

"Sorry, we can't walk Zuni anymore; it cuts into our day too much."

Uh, really? You are retired and you don't do anything all day— so how can something cut into it?

My heart was hammering; I could feel the blood pulsing in my temples and my hands tightening into a fist. I pounded on the phone and started jamming at the delete button, then threw the whole thing across the room. I stomped around the house, pacing like a wild animal on the hunt.

You fucking people—don't bother saying you want to help! Liars! I don't need you! I don't need anyone! How many people had said, "Let me know if I can do anything for you?" Ha!

You can't count on anyone but yourself.

Glancing at the kitchen cupboards, I wanted to grab the dishes and smash them against the wall, so they shattered into a million pieces – just like me. All the knick-knacks that Mickey and I treasured could go too! The temptation was too great, so I stomped into the bedroom and grabbed two pillows, and slammed them against the wall—beat 'em, beat 'em, beat 'em until they broke apart and stuffing flew everywhere. I wanted to scream until my lungs exploded and there was no breath left in me. *I hate this. I hate this. I HATE THIS!*

Loneliness came crashing in on me. I wanted everyone to feel as miserable as I did.

At least I had my pets. I was grateful for Zuni, an affectionate Australian shepherd who Mickey and I rescued, and Pocco, a colorful and talkative, Red-Sided Eclectus Parrot.

Zuni was my attentive, faithful companion. She was always happy to see me, always listened to me and always laid her head on my knee when I needed comforting. She liked to ride in the car when I had errands to do, and our frequent nature walks lifted my spirits.

Pocco had velvet, emerald green feathers accented by red under his wings. Since he'd been with me for nearly eight years, he learned to talk in my voice. He'd say, "How are ya?" "Hi, babe" "What's going on?" "Hi, cutie." When the doorbell rang he'd say, "Come on in!" He was very entertaining but also challenging since he had a deafening squawk and he liked to throw his food around. Pocco's primary residence was a large cage with the door usually left open so he could climb to the top to play with his toys and ring his brass bell. Sometimes, when I was having a particularly rough time, he'd come down from his perch, waddle up to me in the kitchen, and in a sweet voice say, "Are you OK?" I used to say that to him; now he was saying it to me. I'd burst into tears and cuddle him. "Yes, I am OK. At least I'm trying to be." The three of us used to be the four of us and we were all trying to cope with our loss.

One afternoon, I stood at my kitchen sink, staring blankly out the window. I was methodically wiping the sink with a sponge, back and forth, not really caring if it was clean or not. There are certain freedoms to living alone. Suddenly, I was jarred out of my trance by Pocco's piercing screech. I didn't think much of it since he liked to put his head in the bell and talk to himself. Sometimes he would skid down a shiny, smooth pole like a fireman, by clasping his beak and foot around it. It was quite comical.

But then he began to squawk and scream incessantly. Although this is natural behavior for parrots, when you're on edge, it just fuels the anger. He started in, and I lost it! I shouted at the top of my lungs, "Leave me alone! Shut the fuck up! Shut up, you stupid idiot! I'll kill you!"

I took my sweat-shirt off, wound up like a baseball pitcher on the mound and hit his cage repeatedly while matching his volume. "Stop doing this to me. I hate you! Shut up!" I've never felt so out of control. I struck the cage with such force that I broke the zipper on my sweatshirt. In an instant, I knew that if I kept this up, I would kill him. My arm was raised in mid-air to strike again, but I suddenly stopped, as if some force had grabbed hold of me. I sunk to the floor, rolled into a fetal position, and sobbed. "I'm so sorry my poor little Pocco, I didn't mean to scare you. I'm so sorry, so sorry."

Pocco survived, uninjured, thank God. He knew to cling to the back of his cage, out of my reach. Zuni had scurried to hide in a closet. I felt like an abusive spouse, remorseful and promising never to do it again.

I threw my hands on the back of a chair and hung my head in despair. Would my so-called friends ever realize the hurt they had inflicted? Would they ever feel the intensity of loneliness like mine? Maybe my erratic emotions were driving people away. I didn't yell at people. I wanted to, but I didn't. Thank goodness, that would have made me more out of control than I already felt.

The extent of my fury was a stark indication that I needed serious help. Thankfully, Nancy picked up the phone right away.

Just hearing her voice sent a shiver of relief through my body. She assured me that feeling anger was a normal part of the grief process and that I would have to go through it to move on. Within minutes, I was feeling more stable and less like a basket case.

When I studied Elizabeth Kubler-Ross' Five Stages of Grief in nurses training, I never imagined that I'd be going through them while still somewhat young: denial; anger; bargaining; depression; and acceptance. But it's difficult to recognize the stages when you're experiencing them. Considering that I was still in denial some of the time, I was aware that I had a long way to go.

Nancy spoke in a soothing tone and made quite a few suggestions on how to cope. First, she proposed that we do some writing exercises to help work through my process. To my surprise, it was a great tool to help get through my anger, depression, loneliness and hopelessness. Writing out my thoughts and feelings always helped me. I had been journaling for several years, so answering the questions she gave me helped me work through my feelings.

Then she went into her "psychic" mode. Mickey quickly made his presence known and encouraged me to keep moving on. He was never so happy as when we were together, and he wanted me to maintain the happiness that we shared. "It's your time," he said. "You've always cared for others and now you need to take care of yourself. Write the next chapter of your life," he added. "Stop worrying about finances; you are more secure than you think." I listened with a healthy dose of skepticism, but I was willing to believe such reassuring words. They made me feel better.

Nancy went on to advise that I pray to my ancestors and, also to my Native American spirit guide named Howling Moon. Although initially, I was reluctant to believe I had a spirit guide, she asserted that he walks with me everywhere. He was a tribal elder dressed in buckskin pants with fringe, shirt-less with a decorative band on his upper left arm. Two feathers hung from his headband down over his long graying hair, pulled back with a long piece of leather. I soon began to feel his calming presence sitting beside me whenever I meditated. He told me to be at peace and not worry so much. "You will get through this. Talk to me and your ancestors through your meditations; you will find tranquility." I think of my ancestors often and what they went through to find their way in a new country. They persevered through so much hardship. Their stories inspire me to be strong.

As Nancy and I explored different energies, she brought up a profound connection between me and my sister, Carol. She saw that we had been twin sisters in the 1830-1860's. Carol was born first while I took a while longer. Our mother died while giving birth to me and I had carried that guilt ever since. Nancy said I needed to let it go, that it wasn't my fault. In addition, she disclosed that I have a large aura around me. She said a large aura is good and gives good protection. Again, not knowing whether it was true or not, I would've hated to hear that I have a bad aura.

My entire demeanor shifted while speaking with Nancy. She became my solid rock during the journey of healing. So many of her practices, including journaling and meditating, have been so influential in my growth. She made me feel that I wasn't all on my own, after all.

12
MEETING PHYLLIS

Sedona
December 2007

I formally met my neighbor Phyllis about two weeks after Mickey's funeral when I returned to Sedona from Kansas City. She was just arriving home in her car as I walked by with Zuni. She came across the road to inquire how Mickey was doing. I told her that he hadn't recovered from his cancer and died. Her shoulders sagged and she got very tearful. "I'm so sorry, Rose."

We visited for a while and I gave her my usual explanation of what had happened and how I was coping, or rather, how I wasn't coping. She very kindly encouraged me to join a women's group that met at her house to talk about various aspects of their lives. "Maybe it would be good to connect with people," she suggested. I thanked her but politely declined. I wasn't ready to socialize quite yet. She gave me her phone number and said to call if I wanted to talk, get coffee, or go to lunch.

I had seen Phyllis many times over the couple of years that Mickey and I were living in Sedona, but I had never really engaged with her. Mickey knew her better than I. They often had coffee together since they had a lot in common. Both of them had worked in the fashion industry and had lived in Minneapolis for a time.

Mickey was very friendly and talked with everyone, so naturally he connected with her. He would tell me about their conversations, who they knew, and what stores had closed. They usually met in the morning after I went to work, so I wasn't able to go with them. She was genuinely sad to hear about his death.

After our first meeting, Phyllis and I would regularly cross paths while we were out walking. One day we organically started walking together, then having coffee and lunch fairly often. We talked openly. We learned about our families, mutual friends we knew in town, where we had lived. Phyllis was so easy to talk to and was a good listener, so I could see how Mickey enjoyed her company. We came to cherish our friendship. Even in death, I felt like Mickey was taking care of me.

Phyllis was a tall, thin, statuesque woman with polished, ebony skin and closely cropped, curly, salt and pepper hair—with more salt than pepper. Whenever we spent time with one another, I would look at her and envision an Egyptian woman, her head covered in a Nefertiti-like gold headdress, wearing a gold, sparkly caftan embroidered with bright colors. When I told her that I saw her like that, she laughed and disclosed that people would often ask if she was a healer. Although she shrugged off the notion, I thought she was one in her own way. I couldn't define why I thought this, but I swore that I knew her in a previous life in Egypt. It was an odd sensation; I was someone who was just beginning to learn about previous lives and different ways of perceiving the world. I conjectured that, perhaps, we were sisters in Egypt, as she was like a sister to me now.

I eventually joined the group of women that met at Phyllis' home, but it disbanded soon after. People started going their own way, moving to another town, or became busy with careers. I started making my own plans. Six months later, I was back in Kansas City to be near my stepdaughter and my old friends. Because we had become so close, it was extremely hard to leave Phyllis. But I still felt the loneliness of the loss of Mickey tugging at me. I still saw him in our condo sitting in his chair watching television; I still felt him walking with me on the trails and I still felt him sitting across from me at Starbucks. These constant reminders of Mickey haunted me and filled me with such sadness. The move seemed necessary to help me step forward in my life.

As it turned out, Phyllis left Sedona soon after and moved to California along with her spiritual family of James and Brenda who had also become very dear to me. They would all continue to be a great influence on me.

13
OUR KIDS

Mickey adored his two children, Craig and Meredith. His relationship with both of them was very close and their deep affection was reciprocated. In the beginning, Mickey would ask if I wanted children of my own. Honestly, I had never had a burning desire to have my own children, as some women do. Mickey's kids were my kids too.

Craig is a lot like Mickey in that he is athletic, friendly, and handsome. They had an easy, humorous, and caring love for each other. They spoke almost every day, talking about everything— and I mean everything. They both loved sports so that was a frequent topic; but their conversations ran the gamut. For some reason, they liked to call each other "fart knuckle." I have no idea where that came from, but it stuck. Birthday cards from Craig were hysterical and usually tinged with something crude; Mickey got such a kick out of them. If they hadn't seen each other for a long time, Mickey would hug Craig and kiss him on the lips. A very sweet gesture.

Mickey liked to tell the story of the time when Craig was a teen, and he and his friends got up to some mischief. They ended up fleeing from the scene, but the cops nailed Craig because he had a cast on his leg and couldn't run as fast as the others. The cops called Mickey and acknowledged that they knew Craig was not a bad kid so they would release him. Or if Mickey wanted, his son could spend some time in jail "to teach him a lesson." Mickey agreed to the latter, letting him sweat it out in jail for a few hours. Craig was never in trouble again—lesson learned. The two of them never fought. If they had a disagreement, they would work it out. Since they were both talkers, it came easily to them.

At the point when Craig decided he would like to get married, settle down and have a family, he dated quite a few lovely, young ladies. But none of them clicked until he met Jenn. Craig had come to visit us one weekend when we lived in Minneapolis in the late 1990's As he waited at the airport gate for his return trip to Dallas there was an announcement that his flight had been delayed. In exasperation, he let out a loud, "FUCK!"

It just so happened that a cute, dark-haired girl was sitting behind him and she responded with equal frustration, "No kidding, what the…!"

He quickly turned around and their eyes met. "Uh, guess I'll head to the bar; want to join me?"

"Yes," she replied.

The dark-haired girl was Craig's future wife. Although she was living in Dallas at the time, she was originally from Minnesota and was headed home after visiting her parents. When she and Craig became engaged, they decided to move to KC, Jenn arriving ahead of Craig. Mickey and I had moved back to KC from Minneapolis in 1999. She stayed with us at our home, sleeping on the couch until Craig arrived. We adored spending so much time with Jenn, getting to know her. Mickey's favorite was movie night. One night in particular, we watched the film, *American Pie,* pretty much known as an innocent but sexy comedy romp. At some parts of the movie, Jenn got so embarrassed that she put a pillow over her face to avoid looking at us. It was so funny and endearing. Mickey loved to see her blush. She would always refer to Mickey and me as her "Kansas City parents."

Craig and Jenn got married on Mickey's birthday, July 15th, 2000. From that day forward, no one could possibly forget either his birthday or their wedding day. Craig and Jenn would go on to have two beautiful boys; Sam and Alex.

Meredith was the younger of the two children. Mickey had such a soft spot for her, gushing over her with hugs and kisses every time they saw each other. But being a father to daughters was a whole different experience from being a father to boys. When the kids were preteens, Mickey had "the talk" with each of them. He invited Meredith to sit with him on their cozy, screened-in porch to have a little chat. Although he meant well, I'm not sure that it was the best approach to tell a 10-year old, that boys would talk about her if she was "easy." In fact, Meredith had no idea what he was referring to. He finished with an encouraging call for her to be choosy about whom she dated and to "be careful." Meredith would eventually put all the pieces together, but she would never forget the impact of their "talk." On the other hand, when it came to Craig's "talk," Mickey tossed him a bunch of condoms and told him to go out and have a good time.

Mickey and I had many discussions about why there was such a discrepancy between the two methods. I'm sure Cindy had many talks with both kids too. They were both very involved with raising their children and they both did a great job as parents. Since Mickey and Cindy had been divorced for a few years when I got involved, I could tell there was some tension between them. I told Mickey that they would always be parents to the kids and they needed to get along to set a good example. There would be events involving the kids and eventually weddings and grandchildren. They finally had a big talk and were able to work through their difficulties. I think it helped to talk about their issues, as eventually I saw a warming in their relationship.

Meredith had always taken a real interest in fashion, and when in high school and college, loved to "shop" in Dad's closet. At the time, it was trendy to wear baggy apparel, so Mickey's sweatshirts, wool shirts, and jean jackets were the perfect fit. He didn't mind at all; in fact, he delighted in it.

While wearing some of that over-sized clothing, Meredith met a blondhaired young man named Blaine who attended the same college as she did in Kansas. Although she insisted for years that they were just friends, the "friends" started dating and ultimately married.

Mickey always came up with silly nicknames for those closest to him, sometimes without rhyme or reason. Meredith's nickname was "Mary Dinkel" which evolved to "Dink" and eventually, "Dinkster." In fact, I still call her Dinkster. Aspects of Mickey always will be with us.

Mickey would have taken such joy in seeing his children and grandchildren thriving. He would have been so proud of them.

14
MOVES

Minneapolis, Kansas City, Sedona

After six months of settling into blissful married life in Kansas City, Mickey's company sent him to Minneapolis to help increase sales of merchandise in their client's stores. He journeyed back and forth for several months and had great success—so much so, that his employers asked us to relocate there.

Neither of us had any objections to the move as we thought it might be an adventure. I never had trouble getting a nursing job, so I contacted the hospital I trained in and quickly found a position I liked. Another benefit was that we'd be living closer to my family and we'd be able to see them more often. Mickey and I had several discussions about where we should live. I wanted the suburbs, but he had his heart set on living downtown. He asked if we could try his way for a year and, if I didn't like it, we would find a place outside of town. I'd say it worked out well since we flourished in our downtown apartment for eight years. We lived on the 19th floor of a high-rise building surrounded by nice restaurants, sporting events and theater, all bustling with activity. We had lived in our apartment for one month when one day we started having an early snowfall. At first it was beautiful, but it kept snowing and snowing. Between October 31-November 2 we got 28.4 inches of snow. Mickey looked outside at the snow that fell on the city and said, "You mean to tell me I may not see a blade of grass unitl the spring?" I said, "It might happen, but it probably won't." I know he wondered why we had moved here. We felt very secure in our apartment but occasionnally we could hear the cracks of gunfire. Mickey's joke he would repeat to people was, "We can hear gunfire from our apartment—so much so that I can now tell the difference between an AR-15 and an AK 47!" Of course he couldn't but he got a kick out of telling people that joke. Living in downtown Minneapolis would turn out to be a very good move for us. We made lots of friends and excelled in our careers. On the weekends we explored the city on our bikes, went to the gym and attended concerts and sporting events and found great restaurants. Life was good.

Conveniently, Mickey's office was situated in the building adjacent to our apartment. He found much gratification in his work and being amongst so many people. As was typical, he knew everyone in his office within the first two weeks. One of his colleagues mentioned that he had worked in the building for three years and barely knew anyone. But that was Mickey. He talked to everyone and made friends instantly.

Mickey's children visited frequently, and life moved on. A few years passed, Mickey's daughter Meredith got married and a couple of years later called us with some wonderful news. Jaiden was our first-born grandchild, so every little thing he did was a big deal. So much so, that being near to him was the impetus for our move back to Kansas City from Minneapolis when he was just a few months old. Mickey had always said that he didn't want to live "tied down to where his grandkids were." But when the grandkids started coming, he wanted to be near them. We had the joy of experiencing so many of Jaiden's firsts: first tooth; first crawl; first roll-over . When he took his first steps, we celebrated like it was the event of the century. It happened on Halloween when he was about 14 months old. All six grandparents had gathered in Meredith and Blaine's home: Mickey and I; Cindy and her husband Bill; and Blaine's parents, Charlene and Jim. All of us were cooing and playing with Jaiden, unable to take our eyes off our dear baby boy. Something inside of Jaiden must have sensed that he had a captive audience, and he should seize the moment. Because without any indication, he simply stood up and started walking. We were so excited that we cheered and laughed and encouraged him to walk again and again, as if he was a great stage performer. The fact that he was also wearing his Halloween costume lent to the theater of it all.

As Jaiden grew and started to talk, we would say "hat on" and he'd put his hat on and "hat off " and he'd take it off. Then we advanced to "light on, light off." It's an amazing process to watch a baby grasp concepts and gain understanding. And we certainly had fun finding different ways to communicate with him. We always said, "Want me to hold you?" It was so precious when he began saying "hold you" with his arms up in the air when he wanted a cuddle.

I loved spending time with Jaiden, but it was important for me to continue working. So I sought out an administrative opportunity in Kansas City by responding to an ad in one of my medical journals. I interviewed and was hired. Everything seemed to be flowing easily—our marriage was solid, and our family was expanding.

Mickey's son, Craig, got married, and a couple of years later he and Jenn had their first child, Sam. A couple of years after that, Craig was offered a career opportunity. He and Jenn had their second child and a few months after Alex was born, they moved to Philadelphia. Meredith was pregnant with her second child, a girl.

We had returned to the welcoming embrace of our many KC friends and family, both of our jobs were going well, and we were happy.

When Meredith gave birth to CaiLyn, there was lots of excitement welcoming the first girl into our family. I was working at the hospital where Meredith was in labor. Blaine and I were in her room, but things were calm, so we decided to have lunch in the cafeteria while Meredith rested. Blaine returned to her room and I received a page within 45 minutes that CaiLyn had come into the world. I couldn't believe how fast the delivery had been. It was thrilling for me that, after her parents, I was the first one to hold her in my arms—before any other family arrived. What a sweet moment of connection, taking in the perfection of our newborn baby girl.

Over the years, Mickey developed a tradition of buying CaiLyn cowboy boots for her birthday. Then he would buy me boots that matched. One year it was pink boots, the next year it was red ones. It was such a cute thing for him to do. Every year we would put our boots next to each other's and take a photo: Big boots, Little boots.

I have many memories of Jaiden and CaiLyn growing up. Mickey and I spent a lot of time with them, especially joining them for dinner, often for outdoor grilling. Mickey loved to play with words, so he taught Jaiden to say that we were having "hang-a-burgers" instead of hamburgers. Often, we also would have corn on the cob, but Jaiden couldn't say "corn" so he would call it co-en. It took no time before Mickey started calling it "Cohen—the Jewish vegetable." So, our typical family dinners consisted of "hang-aburgers" and the Jewish vegetable.

Mickey was a big tease and loved to get one over on the kids. He pulled that silly trick where he'd put his finger on one of the kid's chests and say, "Look, you have something on your shirt." And, of course, the kids would look down and he would lift his finger to their nose and say, "Gotcha." The kids always fell for it and we'd all howl with laughter. Mickey also did the "grandpa" thing and say, "Pull my finger." And, of course, they would, and he would make a fart sound that inevitably led to another giggle fest.

One weekend, Jaiden and CaiLyn stayed with us overnight for a sleep over. After a lovely evening together, we got them all cleaned up and ready for bed. We didn't have kids' beds, so we provided them with sleeping bags and created a whole scenario of how cool it was going to be to camp out in our spare room. We lay on the floor and as I read a story that I had promised them, they started to fall asleep. I slipped them into their bags and, in no time, they had drifted off to slumberland.

In the middle of the night, we were startled awake by CaiLyn calling to us. "Nana, Poppy, come here." I jumped out of bed and hurried to her. "Nana, I pottied in my sleeping bag." Even though she was drenched, I was relieved that it was nothing more than that. I cleaned her, dried her, and brought her to our bed. "You can sleep here tonight." Before we knew it, Jaiden had also climbed in with us. It didn't end up being much of a camp-out, but boy, we all got a great night's sleep—all snuggly and comfortable together. We always found the kids to be very cuddly, a testament to the affection that their parents had given them.

15
DRAW TO SEDONA

Over the years, Mickey and I had vacationed in many different states in the U.S. but, as we entertained thoughts about retirement, we wanted to make sure that we would find our "utopia." The thought of retiring was strange, but sublime, and we were open to all possibilities.

So, we traveled the country "trying out" different areas. Florida—too humid and lots of bugs, East Coast—too many people, California—just didn't like it there. Arizona—ah, yes! We had stumbled upon Sedona and started vacationing there to the exclusion of everywhere else. Sedona met all the criteria we were looking for in a retirement community. We could take lots of hikes, and it was close to a big city (Phoenix). So, if we wanted more activities (sports, theater, and shopping) we could easily drive to them. We put the wheels in motion. I had been at my job for five years in Kansas City—it was a great job, but once again, I was ready to make a change. Mickey was 60 and eager to retire. Before long, we were having serious discussions about moving and building our dream home, before we got too old to take pleasure in it.

I was insistent that if we really wanted to make a commitment to living in Sedona, we should buy some property. So we did; we bought a condo. But the idea of a dream home persisted. We took the plunge and also bought an acre of land for "someday." At long last, we were on the path to making a permanent move to our little slice of heaven. It was incredibly difficult to part with our friends and family, especially our sweet grandkids. I also mourned leaving my job and brilliant co-workers. But, ultimately, we decided that it was for the best.

All one must do is move a few times, to recognize all the junk we carry around with us and how much we don't need. Our attempt to transfer a 2800 square foot four-bedroom home into a 1350 square foot, two-bedroom condo, didn't go so well. We thought we had edited many of our possessions but determined that another round was necessary. We rented a storage unit; I started a new job, and Mickey retired. We had taken the first steps to reaching our goals.

Retirement was not the easiest transition for Mickey. At first, all he did was watch TV and walk the dog. He quickly got bored and longed to interact with people again. As he was an extrovert, a friend suggested that he inquire about working at the Sedona Chamber of Commerce. He started volunteering, then was offered a paid position. It was the perfect job for such a social person. He stood at the doorway and talked to whomever walked by. If they entered, he would ask what they were interested in doing—hiking, dining, jeep tours—then directed them to the proper person for more details. He loved it.

Having been in the clothing business most of his life, Mickey took his dress for success model to a whole new level at the Chamber by creating job appropriate outfits for himself each day. One day he'd don hiking gear: shorts, hiking boots and shirt. The next day would call for a cowboy outfit: denim shirt with a kerchief knotted at the neck, jeans, cowboy boots and a Stetson on his head. He called himself the "Yiddisha Cowboy." A typical Sedona resident wearing jeans and a southwestern shirt was part of his repertoire as well as a casual tourist look in shorts and a t-shirt. He was having a blast.

On the other hand, I was not having a blast. A 60-mile round trip commute to work, up and down the winding, canyon road, was slow and tedious. I'd often trail behind tourists that didn't know where they were going, who practically came to a stand-still in the middle of the road to take photos. At the hospital, I was the only full-time person in my department, so I was expected to stay until all the work was done—which, of course, was never. It would take me an hour to get there, then an hour to get home. I didn't have time to do anything else, leaving at 6 a.m. and returning home at 6 p.m. or later. Sometimes I was even scheduled on the weekends. After a few months, the stress was getting to me. I'd come home upset and crying, "Why am I here? All I do is work. I don't like my boss and don't like my colleagues. I'm never home. I don't like being here because I can't enjoy it!"

Mickey was panicked. "You don't like it here? We put so much effort into getting here and now you don't like it?" He pleaded with me to apply for a position at a hospital that was located nearer to us. If nothing came of it, he agreed we'd go back to Kansas City.

My situation was a bit delicate since I didn't want anyone to find out I was looking for a transfer to the "sister" hospital. But I took a risk and contacted one of the hospital's managers whom I had met at a meeting. After talking for a while, she said that unfortunately there were no openings. I was crushed. Although I was conflicted, I couldn't imagine continuing to function as I had been. Mickey reluctantly agreed to prepare to return to Kansas City. He just wanted me to be happy.

As it turned out, the very next day I got an email from the manager at the sister hospital. Miraculously, a position had become available. One of the nurses had just given notice that she was transferring to another unit. I was ecstatic. The manager asked me to come in for an interview and I was hired.

Everything took a turn for the better. The commute was no longer an issue. I drove along a short and beautiful scenic route and got home at a decent hour. The people I worked with were incredible and I never had to work weekends. It turned out to be one of the best jobs I've ever had. I was finally able to relax and get decent sleep. Things were looking up.

Sedona started to feel like our home, the ideal location that we had desired. Our lives had an easygoing, steady pace. During the week we were busy, but on the weekends, we relaxed. We loved hiking in the natural beauty that surrounded us; we loved the friends that we had made. We loved daily trips to the bagel store and coffee shop. We loved sharing it with family and friends when they visited us from afar. I had time to plan meals and cook, which was something I had always hoped for. My whole body felt calmer and relaxed. We were optimistic and embracing things to come—the next chapter in our lives.

We had been living in Sedona, our utopia, one year when disaster struck and altered our lives forever.

Hi Babe—

I haven't been sleeping very well so I thought I'd try putting your cologne on the pillow—maybe that will help me.

Carmen called today and said a prayer for you. It made me cry. I still can't believe you're not here. I drove home in a daze. I spent most of my time at work today, reading my books on grief. I just can't handle too much these days.

I want to know your spirit is with me, but I can't feel it. I want a sign from you. Are you ok? Are you at peace? I need a sign to comfort me. Let me know I'm taking care of things OK. I have decisions to make in the next few months and I'd like you to help me know that I'm doing the right thing. I need your guidance. We always decided things together and now I have to make the decisions myself: where do I live? Do I stay here or move? Where should I work? What bills to pay? Give me strength to do that. I just feel adrift or like I'm floating through life not totally plugged in. I miss you so much. I know you know that.

16
A JOURNEY BEGINS

Sedona

It was spring 2007. Our life together was turning out so well that sometimes we had to pinch ourselves to realize that we weren't dreaming; it was perfect for us. Before long, we were arranging appointments with contractors, determined to find that one special person who would help us build our forever home.

One day in June, Mickey casually mentioned that he had been experiencing a strange twinge in his stomach area; it had been bothering him for a few weeks. He asked the advice of his best friend, Nick, who was a general surgeon in Kansas City. Dr. Nick thought it might be a bladder or kidney stone and advised him to see a urologist. Mickey, being Mickey, had another friend in KC who was a urologist, and thinking it was probably nothing, called to make an appointment. We figured we could make a nice little trip out of it, visit with Meredith and family, and see what was ailing Mickey, if anything at all.

His urologist friend thought that the discomfort was most likely due to an insignificant growth and told Mickey not to worry about it. However, he did determine that Mickey had a urinary tract infection and instructed him to self-catheterize to make sure that his bladder was emptying fully. It wasn't the most appealing idea for Mickey, but I assured him that, as a nurse, I had done this task hundreds of times and would help him take care of it.

I had a moment of doubt when the doctor told him to wash and re-use the catheters. I thought it was odd because we always used sterile catheters in the hospital. But he guaranteed that it was ok. So, we returned to Sedona somewhat relieved, and Mickey started self-cathing. I suggested that we find a local urologist, in Arizona, so that if an issue came up, we wouldn't have to make a mad dash back to KC.

On our first visit to the urologist's office in Flagstaff, he told Mickey to halt cathing straight away because it was contributing to his bladder infection. Regardless of stopping, Mickey continued to experience discomfort. The doctor eventually decided to perform a cystoscopy, a procedure to explore the bladder. But he couldn't do so until the infection cleared up. That made sense to me.

A few weeks went by and I observed that Mickey had lost some weight. One morning as he stood in front of our bathroom mirror, his ribs were visible. It made me a little apprehensive because he had always carried a few extra pounds on him. I nonchalantly remarked that he looked thinner. "Well that's good," he said. "I've been walking a lot." I thought, okay, he did need to shed a few pounds. But a few more weeks went by and he was noticeably even thinner. I was privately concerned; something didn't seem right. It was now September and the bladder infection had been going on for three months. The doctor had put Mickey on antibiotics; but they didn't seem to be working, so he kept changing up the meds.

One Saturday, Mickey and I were walking up a small hill and he uncharacteristically asked if we could stop because he was out of breath and needed to rest. I had no problem with that, but Mickey was normally so robust, and it struck me as being unusual. But we finished our walk and made it home without incident.

A couple of days later, as he stood in front of the bathroom mirror, I was shocked at how skinny he had become. His ribs were now protruding. I called the urologist and insisted he do the cystoscopy as soon as possible. He agreed to do the procedure the following week in an operating room to keep things sterile.

On October 2nd, 2007 the two of us drove north along a scenic route to Flagstaff Medical Center. On the way, we took in the splendor of the landscape and commented on how fortunate we were to live in such a place. Once we arrived at the hospital, Mickey was whisked off to the operating room and I found myself feeling very alone. How many times in my career had I comforted families in waiting rooms and kept them informed of their loved one's condition? Thousands of times. Now there I was, with no one else, just me.

I fought a feeling of dread as I waited until the doctor finally returned. I could tell by the way he walked that he did not have good news. He looked dark and troubled; there was no smile. He approached me very slowly with shoulders slumped and a very sad look on his face. "How are you doing?" he said.

"Fine, glad you are out of surgery. How's Mickey?"

He suggested that we go to the consultation room to talk about the procedure. We both sat down as I anxiously anticipated what he would say. "Mickey should be in the recovery room shortly," he said shifting slightly in his chair. "I've done lots of these procedures over the years, but this one was particularly difficult."

I sat up straight, fearing his next words. "Why was it so difficult?"

He took my hand in his. "Your husband has a golf ball sized tumor in his bladder, and it looks cancerous."

"Oh my God," I said as tears formed in my eyes.

I was stunned. I knew that something had been wrong, but this… I felt like a train had hit me head-on.

The doctor continued to hold my hand. "I recommend that Mickey's bladder be taken out within a month. But we don't do that particular surgery here; he'll have to go to a hospital in Cottonwood that specializes in it."

"So, there is hope," I said.

"Oh, yes, of course, there is hope. He is relatively young and healthy; there is always hope." And with that, he directed me to the recovery room.

Craig had called me a couple of times to check on his Dad, but he was in Europe for a wedding, and I wanted him to have fun while he was there. I kept it simple: Mickey was out of the procedure and doing well, but we wouldn't know the biopsy results for a week or two. I didn't want him to worry, although I knew he would. But at least it would put off telling him until he was back home.

In the recovery room, Mickey was awake but groggy. How would I tell him? How would I keep a brave appearance while every part of me wanted to crumble into a heap of sorrow? I wished the doctor was able to be with me, but he was already back in surgery.

Mickey could see the sullen look on my face, so he knew something was wrong.

"Mickey—do you feel ok? I have to tell you something that is very difficult."

I paused, insure of how to go on. "The surgeon found a golf ball sized tumor in your bladder"

"Oh my God. Am I going to die? What did he say?"

"No, you are not going to die. He said they can take the tumor out. They do that a lot. But we'll have to go to another hospital."

"What are we going to do? How do we tell the family?"

"We will tell them together. It'll be all right. We'll get through this together."

He was devastated when I told him the news. Questions swirled between us: how the tumor got so big, so fast; would earlier tests have resulted in a different outcome; how do we tell the kids; what do we do from here?"

His voice quivered as he squeezed my hand and searched my eyes for answers. I tried to stay as positive as possible while drowning in a pool of anguish. "We are in this together, my love. We'll find our way."

We had started on a journey of sorts—one with an uncertain destination. When you hear the word cancer, it's extremely frightening. It opens up a world of terrifying thoughts and emotions. Would the road to recovery be short or long? Would we be able to cope with what lay ahead? I felt like we had jumped off a cliff and into space.

17
END DAYS

We returned home to Sedona and kicked into high gear. It turned out that Nick had a contact at the Mayo Clinic in Minnesota. We set up appointments and did internet searches to learn what the removal of Mickey's bladder entailed. Several trips were made to Minnesota to determine next steps. Mayo recommended that Mickey undergo chemotherapy, before having surgery, to stop the cancer from spreading. We dutifully headed back to Arizona to start his treatment, but his persistent fevers and abnormal bloodwork delayed the start of chemotherapy which in turn delayed the removal of his bladder.

Mickey and I were grateful that we had many friends who called frequently. People wished us well and said they were praying for us. It was interesting that, although we were both ambiguous about prayer, somehow the thought of people praying brought us great solace.

I wrestled with existential thoughts, both enlightening and disturbing. Maybe our experience would lead Mickey and me to a deeper understanding of life, health and our relationship. I decided to journal so that every nuance would be captured.

Meanwhile, the months passed by and, before we knew it, we had entered December. Hospital visits had become more frequent. Mickey was extremely weak and had no appetite. In spite of all the care and medication he was receiving, he wasn't improving. He couldn't climb the stairs to go to bed. He often fell when he tried to walk to the bathroom. I couldn't leave him on his own.

I was so frightened. Helplessly, I watched as my husband deteriorated, fading away right in front of me. The tumor grew exponentially until it was so large that it burst through his bladder into his colon. We rushed to the Medical Center in Cottonwood where I elicited the help of the best surgeon on staff to do a colostomy. The hole needed to be repaired to stop stool from leaking into Mickey's body. I felt like we were in the eye of a tornado that wouldn't stop spinning. Things kept going from bad to worse. "Just make him better," I pleaded with the surgeon.

The operation took place at 10:30 at night. Craig and Meredith were unable to get to Arizona in time for the procedure. Once again, I waited alone. Once again, the surgeon came out, shoulders slumped, no smile, and a very troubled look on his face. Mickey had been put on a breathing machine in the ICU. I knew the outlook was bleak and I desperately wanted to get him back to Kansas City to his family. I was exhausted caring for him by myself and I needed some help if he was ever going to have a chance at getting better. We had been told that the removal of Mickey's bladder was crucial to his survival, yet that had still not taken place. If he were to recover, it would be a long road to get there. I didn't feel strong enough to handle everything on my own. I thought Mickey needed the support of his family, too; he just didn't realize it. I made the decision to fly him by air ambulance back to Kansas City.

My heart ached for him. He was in the wars—not only battling cancer, but cut open, a port in his chest for medication, a breathing tube in his throat and on a respirator.

I stayed overnight with him in his ICU room. I knew I wouldn't get much sleep with doctors and nurses coming and going but I couldn't bear the thought of leaving him. Although he was sedated, he woke for a few minutes and I explained the situation. I looked into his eyes and held his hand. "We will get you better," I said. "I need some help so I will get us back to KC somehow. I love you."

"I love you too," he whispered, and closed his eyes. I didn't know at the time that these would be the last words he would speak.

The next couple of days were a blur. Mickey continued to be sedated and was no longer cognizant of what was going on. I was frantic to get him back to KC. I felt like we were a double act balancing on a tightrope: one false move and we would plummet to certain defeat.

There was a flurry of phone calls as the case manager at the hospital and a close friend of mine tried to arrange for an air ambulance. Once booked, Dr. Nick helped us to secure a bed in the ICU. But, later that day, the hospital called to say that there were no available beds due to an increase in surgeries. I wanted to scream! Should I cancel the flight? Should I tell the kids? We had already been back and forth on the phone several times. I was overwhelmed with important decisions—ones that Mickey and I would normally make together. Sheer panic filled me. I didn't want him to die in Arizona with just me. I wanted his kids, family and friends to be near, the way Mickey would want it.

The next day I woke to persistent worry. The morning crawled along as I waited for answers. Mickey was slipping away; perhaps not much time remained. But during the late afternoon, the phone rang. Nick was on the other end confirming that he had secured an ICU bed for his friend. Relief flooded my body. I was struck by the dichotomy of my emotions: I was devastated that Mickey could be nearing the end of his life but still hopeful that he would survive.

The Air Ambulance arrived at the airport on schedule. To make things easier, Mickey's doctor had decided to keep him sedated and on a respirator for the journey. The crew, which consisted of a paramedic, a nurse, and a pilot, gently settled Mickey in. Since the plane was so small, I was only permitted to take one suitcase. My immediate thought had been: how do I figure out what to pack for two people? When Mickey gets better, he will need clothes for rehab. But a more disquieting thought plagued me… .

The crew placed me in a seat facing Mickey, close to his head, as the plane rolled down the runway. I kept looking at Mickey to make sure that he was OK. As we became airborne, I rested my head on the window. Exhaustion had overcome me, and I promptly fell asleep.

The plane touched down in KC where transport was waiting for us. It felt like I was living in an alternate universe. Was this actually happening? But reality soon set in as Mickey was loaded into the ambulance and off we went. Mickey was greeted by Nick and promptly admitted to the ICU. I was happy when a brilliant nurse, who I had worked with in the past, entered the room to attend to Mickey that night. He would be in very capable hands.

When Meredith arrived, I felt like I could breathe again. Her mere presence filled me with comfort. She embraced both of us and spent a few moments with her father. How I wished that he would awake. He was resting peacefully as we slid out. I needed a solid night's sleep.

Over the next couple of days, Craig and other family members gathered to be with Mickey and offer prayers and support to each other. It was consoling that he was among many loved ones, if only for one last time. We had to curtail the number of visitors because Mickey had developed a systemic infection. I wasn't sure how much more he could endure. The mood was somber, but

I clung to the words of the doctor we had visited in Flagstaff, "There is always hope."

On the third day, those hopes were inextricably dashed. The doctor caring for Mickey asked to see me and Craig and Meredith privately. We braced ourselves for what was to come.

The words that he spoke hung in the room with solemn certainty.

"The cancer has spread all over Mickey's body and into his brain. He will never recover and never breathe on his own. We have done all the tests that we can do and had several consults from other doctors to get a good perspective on what we are dealing with. Unfortunately, the cancer is in his chest, organs, and brain. He will never recover, there is nothing more we can do for him."

"Oh my god... I thought he would recover," I said.

"No, he won't. I'm so sorry. You will have to talk between yourselves and decide what you want to do."

I was crying and so was Meredith. With tears in his eyes, Craig said "He wouldn't want to live like this on a respirator. That's no life."

"I agree, he wouldn't want that,"I said.

The doctor said "Do you want us to take him off the respirator, or would you like more time to talk it over?"

Although the thought of disconnecting him was horrifying, it was even more distressing to think of my dynamic, vibrant, beautiful husband reduced to this way of being. I knew that he wouldn't want to be kept alive on a machine with no quality of life. We had talked about it in the past, never believing the situation would materialize. But he had written clear instructions in his Living Will. One of my jobs in nursing was to help patients complete their Living Will and Mickey and I both had made out ours a few years earlier. Meredith, Craig, and I had another private discussion and made the agonizing decision to take Mickey off the respirator. It was time to release him from the pain of this cruel existence. The children and I sat by Mickey's bedside waiting for the inevitable. Six agonizing hours later he stopped breathing. He died December 15, 2007.

Journal Entry
JANUARY 25, 2008

My Dearest—

Tonight, I went to Pizza Heaven with Tony and Ann. Terri— our favorite waitress felt so bad when I told her about you. David (the owner) came over also. You made such an impact on people.

Then Nick called tonight. He sure wishes he could talk to you— but instead he talks to me. He said he thought I helped him tonight. He keeps bringing up "what if's." It's really irritating because I think we did what we thought was the right thing to do. I certainly didn't want you to die, so I made what I thought was the best decisions. If I keep going over things with, "maybe I should have" it will drive me crazy. I did the best I could—who would've thought you had such an aggressive tumor? I can drive myself crazy with this. Anyway, I noticed a penny on the table when I was talking to Nick. Is that you? I keep looking for signs. I want to know you're alright. Please let me know.

I find myself daydreaming at work and reading passages out of my grief books. It's tough thinking of the future without you. I have no idea what will happen. You are the light in my world. I think about you constantly and miss your touch. I am putting your cologne on the pillow so I can breathe in your scent and think about you. I hope it gives me good dreams of you. You are the best thing that ever happened to me. You have made me a better person by your example. I'll never love another as much as I love you.

18
CHANGES AND BACK TO KANSAS CITY

Sedona

One morning, three months after the funeral, I woke up feeling a desperate need for change. It ran the gamut, but it started with the furniture. As I looked around the living room and bedroom of our home, I thought, this just doesn't fit anymore. I couldn't bear looking at Mickey's chair, envisioning him with his feet propped up, chin resting on his right palm, relaxing as he watched TV. I was sure that Zuni felt the same way as she curled up in that chair each night to sleep.

Having bought much of our furniture years before, I knew it had run its course. So, I purchased a new chair and sofa and decided that I'd donate the old furniture to a local charity. A sudden sadness descended upon me. It felt like I was discarding a part of us, almost as if I was betraying Mickey.

Without a doubt, refurnishing was a good thing, a step forward, so why did I find it so challenging? I went upstairs to the bedroom and looked around. My eyes rested upon our ugly plastic dressers. We definitely could have afforded something better; but there they were, and they had always driven me crazy. I had wanted to replace them when Mickey was alive, but it never happened. What had we been waiting for? So, I purchased a dresser and end tables for the bedroom as well. It was great to get rid of the plastic—a small victory, like I was moving on a little.

Slowly, I began to pack up some of the home "decorations" that Mickey had been fond of. His prized possessions were a worn saddle, some fake rifles, and old native-design quilts. His daughter called it his "crap." I picked up the tattered saddle. It was dusty and had a slight musty smell. As I placed it in the donation box, a landslide of memories came crashing down and I was flooded with emotion. Mickey had been so excited to move to the southwest and decorate our home in the local style. His smile haunted me as tears streamed down my face. One step forward, two steps back. I just couldn't pack up anymore, so I packed it in.

I poured a glass of wine and sat on my patio, gazing up. When I looked to the night sky and the full, bright moon beaming down, I knew it shined on Mickey's grave in Kansas City, too. I knew that the same stars above provided a blanket over both of us. I knew that I was connected to him and it comforted me. I found it painful to accept that he was existing as an entirely different being somewhere else in the universe. We had been so close. The thought of never seeing or touching him again consumed me. I was trying to find my way as a half to our whole. But deep inside, I knew that it was time for me to be whole without him.

Eventually, I got somewhat accustomed to him not being around. I settled into a routine and stayed occupied. I just kept plugging away, aware that I had to do everything myself: pay bills, walk the dog, and make meals for one. But honestly, I still expected that he might walk through the door one day.

Time seemed to move slowly and yet I was surprised that four months had already passed, and our anniversary was approaching. I recalled one year when we coincidentally got each other the same anniversary card. It was while we were vacationing in Arizona, well before we moved to Sedona. I got my card in Minneapolis and Mickey bought the same one in Cottonwood, Arizona. We really laughed about that. We were always so in sync with one another. I tried to be cheerful remembering the good times.

On occasion, I held up fairly well. But sooner or later, I would dissolve into tears. My unrestrained crying caused my joints to ache, my fingers to stiffen and my head to drum out a headache like a full throttle thunderstorm. I was incapacitated, an exhausted blob. Yet sleep eluded me. I found little escape from the heaviness weighing on me.

As I thought about the direction to take going forward, I wrestled with the notion of returning to Kansas City. It was important to believe that I was making some progress, but I was indecisive. The life I'd constructed was stagnant, but it was comfortably familiar. What if I ventured beyond my comfort zone and it did nothing to raise my spirits? I was gripped by fear of making a wrong choice. After a trauma, it is often advised not to make major decisions for at least one year. But that thought was scarier to me than anything else. I couldn't consider being at a standstill for a year.

Indecision plagued me for a few more months, but as I contemplated the pros and cons, I resolved to go back to Kansas City. Despite the hassles of undertaking a move on my own, I had a well-established group of family and friends there, as well as my cherished book club. I was confident that I could stay busy, and that made me happy. At first, things seemed to fall quickly into place as my previous hospital employer said that they would create a position for me. An apartment complex near my stepdaughter Meredith, informed me that they had an availability. I started to feel excited about the possibilities for my future.

Looking around the condo, I immediately bundled some pictures, knickknacks and a pile of clothes to be donated. But things abruptly churned to a halt. First, the hospital stopped being in touch, then I found that the apartment I had inquired about had been rented. I questioned if I was doing the right thing. I certainly didn't want to force my position. I had begun to realize more and more, that life doesn't always happen on our desired timeline, but it eventually works out. I relaxed into the situation and waited for my next steps to unfold. I thought if I was supposed to stay put, so be it. I stopped trying to control things and instead followed the way of least resistance.

As it turned out, I made my move to Kansas City eight months after Mickey's death. As far as I was concerned, that was close enough to the recommended year of no change. However, my enthusiasm for stepping into a new reality was fused with mixed emotions. I would miss Sedona and the beautiful friends that I had made there. Initially, I was so detached from my own decisions, I wondered if it was just part of the grieving process. Although it was difficult, I was determined to make the best of it.

Fortunately, a different hospital job had come through with ease and I was grateful to find an apartment right across from where Meredith, Blaine, and the kids lived. But I struggled to keep myself occupied. At least during the week, I was working at the hospital, but weekends were awful. It was horrendous being without Mickey. I felt empty and bored. I walked a lot, tried to read but couldn't concentrate. Sometimes, I would call Meredith's house to see if anyone was available to meet me at the bagel shop. She was often at a gym class, so Blaine would bring the kids and we would have a bagel together. I also joined them for dinner quite frequently. They could never know how much that meant to me. They were my lifesavers.

If I had little projects in my apartment, Blaine and Jaiden would come over to handle them. Blaine was teaching Jaiden how to fix things. It was wonderful to see how he instructed Jaiden to use tools and complete projects.

After a month in Kansas City, my loneliness persisted. I was disappointed that I wasn't feeling better. Deep down, maybe I thought I would somehow find Mickey there. But of course, that was impossible. A part of me was missing and I was terrified.

Immobilized, I viewed my existence through a distant haze.

I mulled over a single thought: what was my purpose in life now?

19
VALENTINE'S DAY

Kansas City, February 2009

Loneliness pervaded my days, and the nights were torturous. Meredith had made many attempts to distract me from my pain and keep me occupied since Mickey's death. But, as much as I appreciated her efforts, heartache persisted. Fortunately, I was back working at the hospital and that helped me to establish somewhat of a routine.

As Valentine's Day approached, I was filled with dread. But an invitation from Mickey's ex-wife, Cindy, for Valentine's brunch, brightened my mood. Cindy and I always had gotten along; there never was any competition between us. Over the years she became more like a sister to me. There was an ease to our relationship. We could talk about anything and I felt safe with her.

When I arrived at the house, she opened the door and gave me a big hug. "How ya doing, girlfriend?"

"I'm fine, Cindy. How are you doing?"

"Well, I'm doing OK. The kids are here and there's lots of noise, but the food is almost ready. Come on in."

Cindy and I would have coffee together occasionally and we would talk about life, the kids, the grandkids, work, Mickey. It was always a nice get together. Throughout the years we would talk about issues that we weren't sure how to handle. We would ask each other "What do you think?" "What would you do?"

The whole family had gathered, so it was quite a crowd. There was lots of hustle and bustle: talking, laughing, kids running up and down the stairs. As much as I tried to enjoy the atmosphere, I felt a cloud over my head. Mickey and I had visited Cindy often together, but this was the first time that I was there alone, without him.

Several of us were in the kitchen preparing food and chatting, while organizing a beautiful buffet. Scrambled eggs presented in a festive flower dish was the main fare, with bagels arranged on a platter; cream cheese, capers and onions garnished the lox, and a large, glass pitcher of orange juice.

"OK, time to eat, everyone," Cindy called out.

Everyone drifted toward the buffet table. My stomach rumbled but I had no appetite and waited a few minutes before getting my food: a modest scoop of eggs, half a bagel and a small glass of juice. All the kids headed to the living room to be on their own as the adults entered the dining room to sit at the table. I randomly picked a seat. The rest of the chairs started filling and soon everyone was eating and engaged in lively talk. With my fork almost to my mouth, about to eat my eggs, I looked up and saw that I was facing a large mirror behind the table. In an instant, I was reduced to trembling. Every single chair at the table was occupied except the one next to me. It was empty! It hit me so hard—I was alone. My throat went dry and my face flushed. Why didn't someone think to sit next to me? My chest tightened and my emotions welled up. I was desperately trying not to cry and make a scene.

Someone asked me a question in the middle of my panic.

Hardly able to speak, I said, "What?" in a very irritated voice. She asked again, but all I could muster was, "I don't know."

She must have thought I was incredibly rude, but I couldn't talk; my throat was closing. I needed to get out of there. Excusing myself, I went to the living room amongst the kids and sat in a chair. They were absorbed in themselves and I knew that they wouldn't bother me or notice that I was upset. It wasn't long before I told Cindy I wasn't feeling well and wanted to go home. I said a quick goodbye to everyone and left.

On the drive home, I was struck by the clear reality that I wasn't ready to socialize. Happy people and cheerful parties were a stark reminder of the pain that enveloped me. Tears blurred my vision as I peered through the windshield, an all too common occurrence. There were times that I had to stop along the side of the road to compose myself or just have a long, hard cry. What else do you do when you feel so out of control?

I wondered if I would ever feel normal again.

20
SOMEWHERE IN MY THOUGHTS

Kansas City

After a long, exhausting day at work, several months after Valentine's Day, I walked through the front door, tossed my keys on the entry table, and plopped my purse next to them. I trudged into the living room and sank heavily into the comfort of the sofa. As my head relaxed into the cushion, my thoughts turned to Mickey. My eyes dropped closed as I slipped into a daydream of a holiday we had taken in St. Martin years before.

I could almost feel the heat of the sun on my face and the warmth of Mickey near me. We had been looking forward to our big trip for months and were so excited to finally touch down on the runway. We landed on the Dutch side of the island, but we were staying on the French side. Amazing that such a little island, 30 miles across, could have a Dutch speaking and a French speaking side separated only by a small road.

As we departed the plane, we wondered how we would get to our resort. Within seconds, we were approached by a young man who asked if we needed a taxi.

"Yes, we do," Mickey replied. "Can you take us to Hotel L'Esplanade?"

"Yes, sir, I certainly can. My pleasure." He placed our luggage in his truck and off we went.

As we looked out the window of the vehicle, we were amazed to see hurricane damage from a storm that had taken place nearly a year before. Boats were still flipped upside down in the water; planes were tipped on their sides and debris was scattered along the sides of the road. It was kind of scary. We asked the driver why there was still so much wreckage. He said, "This is a poor country, and many could not rebuild." We noticed that some of the resorts we passed were in shambles and closed, but he assured us that our hotel was in fine shape. He also informed us that many restaurants had not yet reopened. Mickey gave me a look as if to say, I hope we didn't make a mistake coming here. At that point, we had no choice but to make the best of it.

We pulled up to the hotel after a 45-minute drive and were relieved to rest our eyes upon a beautiful, sprawling, white building set upon a hill. It's sweeping staircases, accented with powder-blue, reminded me of a huge plantation you'd see in films like *Gone with the Wind*. Lush green trees surrounded the building, palm trees swayed in the breeze and flowers were scattered everywhere. Splashes of red, yellow, and white roses filled the air with a soft perfumed scent. It was a tropical paradise!

We climbed the red brick staircase to the front desk. Everyone we encountered was incredibly pleasant as we checked in and were taken to our room. When the door swung open, we were shocked. The space was huge and even included a second floor. We eagerly walked up the dark wooden steps to the spectacular master bedroom. A large picture-window looked out over the stunning, blue sea. It was breathtaking. I felt like a kid as I rushed around a corner to explore the bathroom. "Whoa, look at this shower!" I shouted. It was so gigantic that I think we could have fit twenty-five people in it. I had never seen a shower without a door, but it did have a window placed on the upper part of a wall. I wondered why it was there. In preparation for our night out, we stepped into the shower and thought why not open the window? A soothing, warm breeze blew in from the sea and light danced on the walls.

We quickly dressed and got recommendations from the front desk for a few restaurants within walking distance. As we strolled down a narrow road that led to a small village, we marveled at the vibrant hues of the women's dresses and head coverings adorning their braided hair. We'd learned about the island's troubled history of European settlers bringing people from Africa to serve as slaves. In the course of time, the Europeans and Africans intermarried, resulting in the mix of hair and skin color. It was a lovely, distinct look that we had never come across before. Eventually, we savored a delicious meal in a quaint French restaurant that was very accommodating to our dietary needs.

The next day we enthusiastically headed toward the beach in our swimsuits with towels flung over our shoulders. Suddenly, to our astonishment, we were surrounded by naked people. We hadn't been told that next door to our hotel was a nudist colony, and the only way to access the beach was to walk through it. Well, the jokes started flying between us. We watched as one naked couple began a nonchalant conversation with another couple laying on lounge chairs. The couple on the lounge chairs had to look up at the other couple. It seemed like an odd angle to us; but it wasn't our business, so we just kept walking, giggling as we passed.

It wasn't long before we became aware that the beaches on the French side of the island were clothing optional. Not that we had any intention of walking around naked, but it added an element of curiosity. Mickey and I found chairs on an uncrowded section of the beach and settled in. We kept our suits on, but lots of other people didn't. At first, it was quite shocking for us to see so many naked people lying around, and we found ourselves people watching in a whole new capacity. One middle-aged man really amused us as he strutted by in a Speedo. His bathing suit was so tiny that you could barely see it due to his huge gut hanging over. He was very tan with dyed black, curly hair and wore a Mr. T "starter set" around his neck: several gold chains with a big medallion hanging in the center of his chest. He was a sight to see walking next to his wife, girlfriend, niece? Whoever she was, she wore a teeny-weeny bottom and seemed immensely proud of her naked, perky boobs. We had a good laugh about that.

The following day we rushed to our spot again, eager to start our people watching. We both opened our paperbacks and tried to read, but we were constantly distracted by the entertaining, "au naturel" characters on the beach. Once we got back home, Mickey joked that when he was reading on the beach, it took him three days before he realized that his book had been upside down.

As we ambled through the sand one morning, we heard a group of young men howling, hooting, and sounding like they were having a great time. We glanced over at one of the cabana bars and saw five guys who were already drunk at 10:30 in the morning. The bartender was a tan, topless woman about their age. It was a simple formula. We looked at each other and had another good laugh.

Later that day we went for lunch at a restaurant on the beach. It was a casual pizza place and we took a seat by the "open air" side: no windows or screens, just a light breeze sweeping through. As we finished giving the waiter our order, we all noticed a young lady approaching the restaurant; of course, she was topless. Mickey teased the waiter, "Not a bad view, huh?" The waiter chuckled and agreed that he didn't mind working at a restaurant with such awesome sights.

We had a nice, light lunch of pizza and iced tea while appreciating the sparkling ocean, swaying palm trees and beautiful flowers. After we finished eating, Mickey, always one to try to speak the native language, took a stab at asking for the check in French. He proudly spouted, "La cuenta, s'il vous plait"—which is half Spanish and half French. The quick-witted waiter replied "Si, Monsieur," and we all roared with glee.

Although we had a dubious start, Mickey and I would remember our time on St. Martin as one of our best. We ate great meals, met some wonderful people, experienced new things and laughed a lot. Mickey's easy, friendly manner always made everything more enjoyable and fulfilling.

As I drifted back to reality from my reverie, I blinked tears. For a few moments, I had been with my Mickey again.

I pushed myself up from the chair, resolving to force myself to do something other than daydream. After all, I had a life to live, whether I wanted to or not.

Journal Entry
JANUARY 27, 2008

My Dearest Love—

Sunday is a hard day for me. It just seems so lonely. I did, however, sit in your chair in my bathrobe for a while watching "Meet the Press." Kinda like you on Sunday. It didn't last very long, maybe a half hour, then I got up.

I got lots done today. I worked out, paid bills, and cleared clutter. I did pretty well—you would be proud. I'm tired of clutter; took me awhile, didn't it? I'm trying to keep things neat for me—and for you. I haven't quite gotten the checkbook balanced, though. I'll keep working on that.

Are you coming to me in shiny pennies? There sure are a lot of them around lately. I still want to know that you're peaceful and happy.

I think about you all the time and talk to you in my mind. Maybe it's me that hasn't found peace yet. I just miss you so much. I am taking your good qualities with me and will continue to act as you would toward others.

I am touch deprived. I imagine your arms around me. I miss that so much.

This is a hard period I'm going through now. Please help me through it. I need your reassurance.

You are the best thing that ever happened to me.

21
A WELCOME VISIT

Kansas City

It had been a little over a year since I moved back to Kansas City. My decision to return hadn't panned out as I had hoped, and I was somewhat restless. My job was all right, but not very fulfilling. The comfort that I thought I would find from being with family and friends had eluded me. This was no one's fault. My support system was caring and accommodating, but I just didn't feel settled. I visited the cemetery but wasn't sure why. Out of obligation? Or expectation of attaining solace? I peered blankly at Mickey's headstone, but I was acutely aware that he wasn't there. The hard fact was, he was not in the world anymore.

It thrilled me to no end when my two grandsons visited from Philadelphia, along with their parents, Craig and Jenn. I asked if the boys could stay one night with me at my apartment. Aching to feel Mickey near, I thought this might be the closest I would ever get. They were two and four years old and full of playfulness. We watched TV, played some video games, and ate sandwiches for dinner. There was lots of laughter and good-natured teasing and, before long, it was time to get ready for bed. I was amazed that they could have so much fun simply taking a bath. Pure joy filled me as they splashed and squealed and devised all sorts of silly scenarios. Sam, the older one, was a little self-conscious about his body, so he kept covered up a bit, but the two-year-old, Alex, was not. He ran around without a care and not a stitch of clothing.

Putting their pajamas on was a bit of an adventure as they wriggled and chatted and did everything to avoid the inevitable. At some point, we all climbed into my kingsized bed, since it was the only bed I had. We watched one of their favorite children's program until they got drowsy and Sam rolled over and drifted off. Little Alex fell asleep on my chest. There is nothing quite so beautiful as holding a child and watching them as they sleep. It is something I will never forget. I stayed awake most of the night just taking in the depth of the feeling and, every now and then, grateful tears slid from my eyes. I could have easily collapsed into a full-blown cry, but Alex would have woken, and I didn't want to disturb him. He was so peaceful.

I looked over at Sam sleeping so peacefully and thought about times when Mickey and I would take him out to breakfast or lunch. Mickey would look at the placemat with Sam and point to a picture of a girl.

"What is that, Sam?"

"It's a girl" Sam would say.

"No, Sam, she's a hottie."

Sam would look at us and I'd say "Yup, she's a hottie."

Then Mickey would point to a picture of a girl on a bike. "What is that, Sam?

"That's a hottie on a bike!"

Mickey and Sam would high five each other. Quite amusing.

When you have lost a loved one, something you really miss is contact, the closeness with that person. At long last, Alex had helped me find a connection to Mickey. He was his flesh and blood. My memorable time with the kids seemed to pass so quickly, but I embraced every second. The lack of sleep was worth it. I didn't feel the least bit tired the next day.

22
THE UNIVERSE

Although I had begun my life with a deeply rooted sense of religion, ultimately, going to church didn't give me the sense of comfort that I had hoped for. So, I continued searching, although I didn't know what I was searching for, or even that it was a search. After Mickey's death, when my world became topsy turvy, I found myself thrust further into my quest. While on my grief track, I had experiences that I could never have imagined. They led me to turn from organized religion and consider a combination of beliefs from a variety of faiths.

I first heard the term, "The Universe," while still in Sedona shortly after Mickey's death. It resonated with me immediately. People would say things like, "The Universe is kind. The Universe has a plan. The Universe wants the best for all of us." Wondering what that meant exactly, I kept listening. Perhaps my ears had opened for the first time because it stirred something deep inside of me. The concept felt all encompassing, not exclusive. It applied to ALL beings on earth. Like most people, I wanted the best for myself and my family. I hoped that joy and happiness would fill our days. But I struggled with wondering how I could find such contentment after enduring such a great loss. I had no option. I just kept repeating to myself, "The Universe is kind; it wants the best for all." I read books, talked to friends and people who were different than me, and listened to programs on spirituality on TV and on the internet.

As I continued on my path working through my grief and contemplated that an essence greater than I was providing guidance, I began to heal. At some point, I began to grasp complex concepts, such as how to embrace the universal perception of no judgment and complete acceptance. After all, isn't that what we all desire? This belief system encourages each of us to find our own way. It puts the reins of control in the hands of each individual to create what they want. I found it such a departure from the entrapments of organized religion. For the first time that I could remember, I felt free.

Some use the Universe as another term for god, but for me, it's simply an omnipresent force that guides us—no strings attached. I guess you could say the concept refers to a higher power. I would come to relate particularly to the idea of spirit, angels, and guides. For me, these entities have made their presence known in my times of greatest need. When I thought I had nowhere else to turn, I felt like I received instruction or advice from these powers. This was especially true after Mickey died. I was so used to talking to him and making decisions together, but I slowly learned to trust my gut and trust the Universe.

Lots of energy can be wasted worrying about what is to come. But I have learned to let things play out as they will. I've learned to relax and not worry so much. My daily affirmation is, "The Universe has a plan, and everything will unfold as it's supposed to." As I've progressed in my beliefs, I feel that the Universe encourages us to live to our fullest potential so that we may achieve success. Some of us may struggle to get there. Things get in the way: lack of education; poverty; illness; relationships, among other obstacles. But many people rise up, regardless of their situation, to manifest their dreams.

I began to look at the world in a different light. Enduring devastating challenges changed me, made me move in a different direction. I no longer sought the anchor of a church to hold me in place. Rather, I saw myself as a boat afloat on an infinite sea of possibilities. I wanted to set sail along whatever course the waters took me.

23
GRANDMOTHER RITA

Kansas City

Despite my burgeoning sense of optimism, my days continued to be measured by how long it had been since Mickey's death.

My thinking had become more expansive, and my awareness had increased, but Kansas City was assuredly not Sedona. I was concerned that I wouldn't find a way to nourish the spiritual aspect of me and I would lose ground.

Fortunately, soon after I got to KC, I received an email from my therapist friend Brenda, who had introduced me to Robert, the astrologer. She asked if I remembered her telling me about the Thirteen Grandmothers Council. These women were elders of their indigenous communities. They were often consulted and involved in decision-making for their communities. They traveled around the world talking to groups about issues facing the Earth. Every one of them had a unique story to tell about growing up in their communities, customs, and way of life. I had read a book about each of them and was fascinated with the stories. As it turned out, one of the grandmothers was going to be in Kansas for a session and Brenda highly encouraged me to attend. I vaguely recalled hearing about them, but I was curious. After all, Brenda, James, and Robert had been instrumental in leading me to my new path. My head was spinning a bit as I grappled with the idea of attending what I had considered an "out there" meeting. I was hesitant, but once again took a leap of faith.

Brenda gave me the number of the woman, Debbie, who was organizing the event. She was hosting the event and lived somewhere in the countryside in Kansas. Debbie and I talked for quite a while, and before I knew it, I had agreed to pay the fee. I questioned my sanity, thinking that maybe I was being naïve and might be getting scammed. It was not like me to take such a chance. As I mailed a check to Debbie, I imagined it sprouting wings and laughing at me as it flew away into oblivion, never to be seen again.

The only information I had about the location of the Grandmother event was that it was at a place called The Lighthouse, somewhere in the Kansas countryside. I was put in contact with a couple who lived not far away from me, so that we could carpool. As I made my way to their house, I experienced a growing anxiety and fear. Traveling with perfect strangers was not my idea of a fun time. What would we talk about? What if I didn't like them?

I arrived at their house at 8 am.

The husband was a great big guy who wore self-made jewelry and chunky rings on all his fingers. He seemed friendly enough, but then his wife appeared. She charged into the room with her flaming red hair and barked, "Don't talk to me. I am NOT a morning person."

I became leery. I chastised myself for being such an idiot. Why had I agreed to this arrangement? But there was nothing I could do except ride it out. I had visions of being kidnapped and killed and no one knowing where I was. I kept telling myself not to make assumptions, that there are nice people everywhere; they may just look and act differently.

Reluctantly, I got into the couple's van and we were off. We left the city and rode for about an hour and a half while I sat in the backseat praying that I would be alright. On the final stretch, we drove down a wet, bumpy road until we pulled up to a rickety, wooden structure. We had to slog through thick mud to reach the old building. I would much rather have been at home on my couch with my dog at my side than in this miserable place.

Damp, stale air greeted us as we opened the door. A fresh panic rose in me when I saw how many people had gathered inside. About 50 people, mostly women, but a couple of men were there, mulling around, looking at some tables people had set up with jewelry, crystals, and other items for sale. I didn't know a soul. There was lots of chatter about UFO's and ET's and auras and things that I considered weird. What the hell... what had I gotten myself into? The couple I came with quickly disappeared into the group and I was left by myself, feeling extremely awkward. I had no clue how to talk to these people.

There was no way out because I really didn't know where we were, and I had no transportation. I was trapped. Dread must have been written all over my face, but I tried my best to appear friendly by looking at items that vendors were selling. Inside, I was panicked. I just wanted to get the hell out of there.

After a few minutes, my focus was drawn to two Asian-looking women sitting at a table off to the side. Their distinctive clothing indicated that they might be the Grandmothers. They wore flowered garments and shawls in contrast to the more contemporary and younger garments of the attendees. They sat quietly, observing the crowd.

At long last, one of the women who identified herself as Grandmother Rita from Alaska, invited us to follow her upstairs to start the meeting. One by one, we tramped up the creaky, wooden steps to a room on the second floor of the small house. The steps were so narrow that I thought they would collapse under our weight. Surviving the climb, I immediately spotted a wooden bench and sat next to a young woman who seemed to be by herself.

My heart pounded as I anticipated what was to come next. I had no idea, but I was hoping that it wouldn't be a waste of time, and I would at least learn something. I noticed my red-headed driving companion sitting in a big chair with a crystal in the palm of each hand and her eyes closed. Her husband was nowhere to be seen. I was trying not to make judgments, but I couldn't help thinking about how many odd people were in attendance.

Grandmother Rita Pitka Blumenstein sat calmly in a circle with a few others and began to speak in a soft, soothing voice. She lived in Alaska, grew up in a family of seven children and married a Jewish guy from New York. What an interesting combination and what a coincidence. I also was one of seven children and married a Jewish man. Rita went on to describe her tribe in Alaska and their many customs.

She spoke reverently about a specific incident that had occurred when she was only a little girl. At age nine, her grandmother revealed that when Rita was older, she would be asked to sit on a council consisting of 13 grandmothers, who would do important work in the world. Her grandmother had prepared 13 sacred bundles that contained 13 eagle feathers and 13 stones, which she ceremoniously entrusted to Rita until that time came.

Rita was to keep one bundle for herself and give the others to the remaining women to remind them that their ancestors were present with them. Fulfilling the prophecy, at nearly eighty years old, Rita was a part of The International Council of Thirteen Indigenous Grandmothers, a group of elders who had been brought together by a common vision to form a global alliance to heal the Earth and its inhabitants. Her words gave me goosebumps.

Rita shared many insights and encouraged us to communicate with those who had passed. She suggested that we talk with our elders, pray, take joy in solitude, and pay attention to our inner voice. Wow. I thought she was spectacular. I felt an instant bond with her. Stories that older people told about the past brought me great pleasure. I had always been intrigued with the past, eager to learn more about my ancestors and distant relatives. Admittedly, reaching out to those who had passed was a stretch for me, but I was so impressed by Rita's certainty.

During a break, I let her know how much I enjoyed her, and mentioned the similarities in our lives. She came from a family of seven children and so did I. She married a Jewish man and so did I. She was a widow and so was I. She asked me several questions, mostly about Mickey; then I told her he had recently died. Having also been widowed, she gently asked if I'd be willing to talk to the group about it, while she gave me a healing. I would have loved to have had a "healing," but I couldn't possibly talk to a group about his death – it was still too painful. Rita understood. She thanked me for our interaction, and I returned to my bench. Instead, a young lady volunteered to stand in front of the group to receive a "healing." This ritual consisted of Rita walking around the young lady, beating a drum and singing a song. She chanted some "prayers", I believe, in her Native language. I wasn't sure what it was supposed to do for her; maybe it did cure her. But I didn't believe that Grandmother could repair what was broken in me; the wound was too deep.

Our afternoon was filled with singing, dancing, and additional pearls of wisdom that Rita imparted. A companion from her village, named Marie, demonstrated some of the tribal dances performed at their various ceremonies. Her long, white hair flounced among the large white feathers she held. I was mesmerized by her simple dance as she stepped back and forth and turned round and round in a circle. Afterwards she invited us to play some instruments—rattles, drums, and bells—and we all danced enthusiastically to the music we made.

The next day, I drove to the Light House with the strange couple again. The redhead sat in the same chair with the same crystals and her eyes shut, again. And the husband did a disappearing act, again. And, again, I sat on the bench next to the same woman from the day before. Grandmother Rita shared more about her culture, then drummed for us. The drumming had a strong effect on me. It vibrated in my chest and stirred up emotions, while at the same time, bringing me serenity. Before long, we were all grabbing instruments from a basket, and dancing around the room. Everyone seemed to be having fun.

Throughout the day, the young woman sitting next to me and I talked and got to know each other. It turned out that Anna lived just a few miles from me. She had never been to one of the Lighthouse events either, and she also was on her own. She was in her thirties and I was in my fifties but, despite the disparity in our age, we really hit it off. Within a few weeks, we had become friends. We had lunches and dinners together and spent several hours on the weekends talking on the phone and going to each other's houses. We also attended many more events together at The Lighthouse.

As the day ended, my traveling companions stated that they would not be returning for another session as they hadn't really gained anything from it. I sat in the backseat, looking out the window with a big grin on my face. I hadn't felt so comfortable with my driving partners, but I felt much more comfortable with myself and the many lovely people I had encountered at the Light House. True to my wish, I had learned a lot.

At the onset of the weekend, I had been consumed by fear. But what a weekend it turned out to be. It had been one of the best adventures of my life. The Lighthouse became a "go-to" place for me to delve into these new, foreign experiences. I was fortunate to witness the teachings of several of the other Grandmothers over the coming months. We'd pray together, meditate, experience sweat lodges, receive "healings" and blessings, and experience words spilling from the mouths of channelers. I was so eager to venture further into this Metaphysical realm.

Something had shifted in me. I guess the best way to describe it is, that I had become "spiritually alive." The Grandmothers really resonated with me and I became friends with many of the wonderfully supportive women I met at the Lighthouse. The first time I visited, everything had felt so strange and off-putting, but I had come to deeply appreciate the wealth of knowledge that had been offered to me.

24
GRANDMOTHER AGNES

Kansas

A few months after Rita's visit, I was elated to hear that another Grandmother would be arriving in Kansas. I was still feeling the ripples of my first episode – the beautiful people I had befriended and the awareness that I had gained. Anna and I immediately made plans for another trip to the Light House.

Agnes ("Aggie") was from Oregon where she was a spiritual elder of the Siletz tribe. As she entered the room, I was quite taken by her presence. She was very tall with long, flowing, white hair. Beads and shell jewelry clinked and tinkled from around her neck, accenting a native dress that swept down to the tops of her deerskin moccasins. Her incredible energy was palpable, as she greeted each one of us with the kindest smile I had ever seen.

But the most striking thing about Aggie was that she was covered from head to toe with images of dragonflies. They were attached to her skull cap, socks, dress, fastened to her hair and dangling from her ears. She disclosed that she had placed them all over her house as well—on towels, aprons, curtains and hanging as ornaments from her garden trees. It was no surprise when she divulged that her native name was "Naibigwan" which means Dragonfly, known in her tribe as the "Transformer." According to Tribal legend, when their people pass on, they return, transformed, as dragonflies.

Aggie stressed her belief that the Creator had given us the ability to think, thus it was our mandate to be caretakers to all that came before us and to keep the four elements of earth, air, water, and fire in balance. She lamented that humanity had walked away from primal teachings, and as a result, the planet was suffering. Her firm resolve was to save the planet, with a keen regard for water, which she maintained was crucial for the survival of all living things.

Although we sat in a large circle in a large room, Agnes engendered such intimacy when she spoke. She talked about how culture and tradition were crucial to the identity of her tribe and that respect was greatly valued. One tradition that stood out to me was the role women played in times of war. They were expected to engage as peacemakers with the hope that the men would follow suit. It reminded me of when my own grandmothers talked about living in a small town in Minnesota and how they worked hand in hand with Native American women to help one another during harsh winters. They taught each other cooking techniques, how to store food, and shared whatever food they had with each other. Agnes believed wholeheartedly in the innate perceptions of women. She avowed that the Grandmothers had come from far and wide to speak the knowledge that they held inside and, that as women of wisdom, they could not be divided.

Grandmother Agnes accentuated the value of having vision. She talked about her spiritual journey and how being "at death's door" from a cancer challenge had launched her into a deeper purpose.

"I asked the Creator to let me live because I had much to accomplish in my life. I needed to care for my extended family. I also felt I had much to teach in my country and around the world. I was 45 at the time and I fully recovered, and here I am in my 80's able to talk with you." But a restlessness had been born in her that even crept into her dreams—a knowingness that she would join with other light bringers to be a voice for the voiceless. Her pursuits led to her sight opening beyond ordinary capabilities so that she could psychically see with her eyes closed. "We are going to see change," she affirmed. "If we can create the vision in our heart, it will spread."

I was truly inspired by her confidence and positivity.

After a while, Agnes gently shifted the conversation to focus on the group. She went around the room and asked each person why we had come and what we hoped to gain. I sat attentively while most people talked about their spiritual path and when it had started. We were halfway around the room when my turn came, and I cheerfully began to tell my story. As I disclosed that I had been propelled into my journey a year and a half ago when my husband died, I unexpectedly burst into tears. My face got hot and I shook with emotion. I wasn't sure what happened. I had been doing so well: happy to be there and feeling better. Anna grabbed my hand and put her arm around me. "I didn't want to do this," I mumbled. "I didn't want to cry." My voice was gone, and my head hung down.

Aggie said to me, "Just remember that you are loved."

I hadn't told many people about my loss, but now everyone knew. I felt like a wreck, wrung out, and embarrassed that I had lost control. It was shocking to realize that my pain was still so close to the surface. After we concluded, many women comforted me—some having had a great loss themselves and some just giving a supportive hug. I felt grateful to be amongst people that were so caring and understanding.

That evening, after dinner, we assembled at the campfire with Grandmother Agnes right along with us. Some women drummed; others played their flutes. Agnes sat in a chair and clapped along with the music as we all sang, danced, laughed, and chanted. It was absolutely wonderful to watch an 85-year-old woman enjoying herself so completely while we all let loose and made blissful fools of ourselves.

Grandmother Agnes eventually went to bed, but about 10 of us headed back to the main meeting room and stayed up a while longer. What started as casual conversation quickly morphed into something entirely different. I was caught off guard as one woman suddenly started "channeling" Bigfoot.

"Oh boy, here we go…. what is it with this crowd?"

It was new terrain for me, but I felt safe. I just couldn't understand what was going on. Before I knew it, another woman began to channel one of the Grandmothers. She pursed her lips together, hunched over and talked in a squeaky voice completely different than her own. It certainly wasn't any Grandmother I had met. The woman's husband was also there, one of the few men that attended these events—and he started channeling a leprechaun! He was from Ireland, but I wasn't buying that leprechauns were real. It just seemed so zany to me. Then Anna started channeling a Lemurian, whatever that was. Anna of all people. She and I had become close and she had never given any indication that she channeled. Since then, I have learned that Lemurians are one of the rarest and ancient wisdom keepers of the planet. I don't understand all about them but found the stories about them very interesting—something new again to learn about.

All at once, I thought, "Oh no, I'm going to lose it." I managed to suppress an inappropriate urge to giggle uncontrollably—although it would have been a welcome release.

If everyone hadn't been so serious, it would have been comical. I looked around and thought, am I next? How does this work? Who could I possibly channel? I didn't have the slightest clue what I was doing there. Continuous channeling lasted for almost an hour with a host of beings coming and going. I thought maybe the house was going to get sucked up by a tornado and fly off to Oz. But, eventually, everyone came back to earth and resumed as their normal selves. I couldn't resist asking them why they thought I had been involved in the session. It was perplexing to me because I didn't have the ability to channel. I had simply been a quiet, and somewhat amused, observer. They all agreed that my role had been to keep everyone "grounded." Maybe they were right. Afterall, we didn't end up in Oz, did we? So, I chalked it up to yet another unique, weird happening—but wow, what fun.

Since leaving Sedona, I had been meditating and praying quite a bit. I always asked to be open to whatever was sent my way. I believe that when you are open to new ventures, as I was and still am, they definitely present themselves. I entered a sphere of possibility so different from what I had ever known. I made a choice to be more open to new ways of seeing the world. Although my experiences in Sedona had kicked off my journey, I soon came to realize that there are many people with extraordinary gifts who thrive everywhere you can imagine – someone standing next to you in line, eating in the same restaurant, living in Kansas, Arizona or anywhere else in the world.

Journal Entry
DECEMBER 15, 2009

Pondering a move back to Sedona….

It's been two years since you passed away. How do I articulate how I feel? Where are you? I haven't dreamed about you—don't know why. You haven't visited me in dreams or meditation. Ugh, crazy talk….

It's so sad sometimes because I miss you so much and it seems like the recent past.

Then sometimes it feels so long ago.

It's a very different experience, living alone. There must be a divine plan; I am learning to rely on myself again. I am preparing for the next journey. Well, I'm on a journey already—it's just the next phase.

I don't cry anymore, but I have such a tender spot for you—I always will. All my experiences continue to lead me to my life now. I still don't fully know what my purpose will be, but I continue to be open to all possibilities. I look forward to the time when I don't have to work so much and can devote my energy to something other than the hospital.

So much has changed. Your death thrust me into a whole new world. Why? Why don't I stay the same? Why does everything have to change? I have paid the bills for two years. I've taken over everything you did. It's just me, Zuni, and Pocco. What am I to learn from this uprooting, emotional experience? I ask why all the time.

My anger has subsided into acceptance. I must go forward and live for me. I don't know what that means, but I am constantly searching. I am learning to trust my heart and my gut and let my head be quiet. That is so new for me. I am learning what good friends are and that I am a good friend in return. I am learning to find my teachers and that they are all around. I am self-sufficient and have gotten strong through all of this.

I am told that all my experiences in life have led me to this place. Am I to be grateful to you for leaving so I could learn about myself ? I would never have wished that you'd leave.

Now I must continue forward. I feel like I'm ready to consider a new relationship. Though I will continue to work on my spirituality. I am a different person, and the next relationship will be very different than with you. But I miss companionship. I don't cook anymore, and I miss that. I would like to share duties and take all the burden off me.

I feel like I'm saying goodbye. In a way, I am. It's another layer of letting go and it needs to be done. You will always be in my heart. Our relationship was the best we both had.

I don't know what 2010 will bring, but I am ready. I always keep a higher purpose first and the rest comes naturally. I will always feel your spirit.

25
GRANDMOTHER MARGARET

Kansas

Grandmother Margaret, affectionately referred to as the "Red Spider Woman," led a workshop at the Light House only two weeks after Aggie had been there. A few months prior, I had never heard of the Indigenous Grandmothers, but as time went on, I couldn't get enough of them. Fortunately for me, Kansas seemed to be one of the hubs for their frequent presentations. Anna and I made the now familiar trek along old country roads to the boondocks of the state. I marveled at how comfortable I felt as we approached the Light House—a big change from the bundle of nerves I had been on my first visit.

Margaret hailed from the Arapaho/Cheyenne Tribe of Montana. Clothed in a long, shift-like garment with simple beads around her neck, she dressed more plainly than Rita and Agnes. Her auburn hair was streaked with a few strands of silver and curled like she had slept in rollers. Margaret's serious demeanor accentuated her powerful yet inviting presence.

She talked about how her parents had been migrant workers who had no choice but to leave their eight children to be raised by their grandparents. She stressed that in her culture they didn't have aunts and uncles but rather many mothers and fathers. So, she always felt that she was cared for within a family, even though her birth parents were often absent for extended periods of time.

An accomplished sculptress, author, and traditional dancer, Margaret found a creative outlet in doll making in her later life. Her mother had taught her the fine art of beadwork and how to make buckskin dresses for her dolls. She also imparted the significance of the tribe's sacred designs which she blended into her creations. Anna and I were delighted that she had brought a collection of them with her for display and sale.

Like the other Grandmothers, Margaret shared some of the rituals specific to her tribe. But I was quite taken back when she emphasized the importance of incorporating peyote into their ceremonies and in their lives in general. I am not a drug person at all, and I consider myself a skeptic when it comes to any recreational drugs. I have never thought it was a good thing to experiment with them. It interferes with the way your body functions and I have never had any desire to try them. I saw too many people in the hospital with drug and alcohol issues, so talk about drugs makes me extremely uncomfortable. I verged on paranoia as I feared that Margaret would encourage us to try peyote. I pictured the group ingesting it and the weekend devolving into one long, lazy event with everyone laying around sleepy-eyed and having "visions," something that I had half expected would happen sooner or later because the gatherings were always unpredictable.

As Margaret talked about the benefits of peyote, I wondered how I could make a quick exit. Resentment built up in me as I imagined being "spiritually" persuaded into taking a hallucinogenic. In contrast to my anxiety, Margaret spoke in soft, easy tones about her grandfather building a tipi for her when she was a little girl for the purpose of holding a life ceremony in her honor. He planted prayers in her name and emphasized the relevance of peyote for their people. Margaret claimed that it was a healing medicine that creates a sense of well-being and assists in facilitating rich and colorful visions.

I thought, "I'm sure it does, but it's not for this girl."

She regarded the drug as a spiritual remedy that helps put an individual in touch with the god within, and back into balance with the Earth. Her assertion was: if used correctly, it eliminates the need for other medicines; it's a healing substance that isn't addictive. I'd read stories of Native Americans and some rituals they did to give them a "spiritual" experience, but I really didn't think one could be cured by peyote. I was very skeptical.

I was convinced that she was going to break out the peyote and "heal" us after we all got high. I had a battle going on in my head: should I leave, or should I stay to see what would unfold? But I sensed that my obsessive thinking was in complete contrast with Margaret's intentions, and I had to find a way to shift it. I sat quietly, breathed and tried to be in the moment. After a while, I managed to stop the voice in my head from yammering away so I could listen without judgment. I reminded myself that I could always get up and leave if I was so inclined.

Margaret told many stories of peyote healings—how her mother recovered from a broken hip with a healing ceremony, and how her sister-in-law was cured of Crohn's disease. I had so many doubts listening to her stories. How could peyote possibly cure a broken hip? Crohn's disease is such a complicated, terrible condition. How could peyote cure that?...or a "healing" session? Although doubtful, I remained attentive. I was happy to hear her say that her tribe didn't consider peyote to be a recreational drug and that it's treated reverently, with any abuse being severely frowned upon. It turned out that Margaret hadn't brought any with her after all, so there was no chance that we'd be asked to indulge. I sighed with relief.

While I had become completely preoccupied with the whole issue, I came to realize that Margaret's principal objective was to have the group participate in a sweat lodge. I had no idea what a "sweat lodge" was. I was intrigued, felt comfortable enough, and thought I would like to try it. She encouraged that, if we wanted to partake in it, under her supervision, we were welcome to do so; if not, it wasn't a problem. The concept was presented in such a non-stressful fashion, that I decided to join in. In preparation, she suggested we not eat a lot of food at lunch, and drink plenty of water.

Upon entering the sweat lodge, I had a slight twinge of nervousness. It was similar to a tent but with a sturdier structure. The ceiling was so low that we couldn't stand up. So, we walked in while bent over, and sat in a circle on a dirt floor, loosely covered with blankets. Eighteen of us packed in tightly together. The flap that covered the opening was pulled back to let light in as we got settled. The damp earth floor felt cool beneath our feet. In the middle of the circle there was a pit containing hot rocks and water—kind of like a sauna. Margaret proposed that we pray or meditate while she conducted the opening ceremony of singing songs, relating stories, and saying prayers. If we felt too hot, she advised us to lay our hands flat on the earth to cool down. To alleviate any concerns, the door flap would be opened every so often to allow an exit for anyone who wanted to leave.

Grandmother Margaret sat tall, took a deep breath, and asked if we were ready to begin. There was a resounding yes. The door flap swung closed, and we were immersed in complete darkness. I closed my eyes right away so I wouldn't feel claustrophobic. Margaret threw water on the warm rocks, and they sizzled and smoked as we plunged into unchartered territory. Every time she tossed more water on the rocks, they crackled and sputtered to increase the temperature. Wow, it got hot! Sweat poured out of me, trickling down my face, back, and neck. My shirt stuck to my body and my shorts became soaking wet. But overall, I felt good and at peace. Margret prayed and lightly beat a drum while someone outside the lodge struck a drum as well. The door flap was opened four times during the two-hour session and, although I was tempted to leave, I resisted. Once I got used to the heat and smoke, I fell into a serene, trance-like mode. As I surrendered to the moment, I sensed ancient spirits in the lodge with us. I let myself drift in and out of consciousness while all inhibition drained from me. At one point, I felt a reassuring hand resting on my shoulder. I believed it was Mickey, coming to comfort me. While many of my recent experiences had pushed my limits, this one had transcended my everyday existence into the mystical. It was truly life-altering.

As our time in the lodge drew to an end, Margaret gently coaxed us to find our equilibrium and, one by one, we filed out of the tent without a sound. I waited outside for Anna, eager to hear what she thought. I was alarmed as she stumbled through the open flap, clearly distressed. As I approached her, she cried out, "I can't see."

I advised her to sit down to let her eyes adjust to the light.

She repeated, "I can't see" over and over.

I could tell that she was in an altered state because she was talking in a language I didn't understand. I wasn't sure if she was channeling or not, but I was scared. With urgency, I asked someone to find Grandmother Margaret to come help. She appeared within seconds and instructed us to lay Anna on the ground and straighten her hands and feet. Anna had stopped speaking and was gagging, coughing, and shaking. I was afraid that she would have a seizure.

Grandmother was very calm and assured us that Anna was alright. "Turn her on her side so she can expel whatever is aggravating her."

When we placed our hands on Anna to soothe her, she finally regained control, and her sight also returned.

Anna sat up, acknowledged the six of us who surrounded her, and spoke freely in a channeled Lemurian language. Although I didn't know the language or what she was saying, I was relieved that she was responsive and composed. One at a time, she focused on each of our faces, lovingly caressed them, then initiated a "healing." It was amazing to see how her expression changed with each individual she took in. She smiled affectionately at a younger girl as if she was her child. She beamed at a woman, about my age, who she had recently befriended, as if she had been a dear friend for many years. I was so moved when she came to me, looked deeply into my eyes and called me "my ancient one," a recognition that we had known each other through multiple lifetimes.

As Anna completed the circle, she stood silently for a few minutes until she relaxed into her body. She softly revealed that her "siren" had spoken through her with all the love that she could summon from within. Although Anna and I had become very close, I was not always aware of her other-worldly connections. Nor did I comprehend them. But I approached all of my undertakings as if I were viewing the scattered pieces of a giant puzzle. With time and contemplation, I was certain that they would fall into place and a bigger picture would emerge.

Each of my encounters with the Grandmothers had been a compelling adventure in its own right. As always, the different combinations of people led to varying conversations and interests, as well as deepened relationships. It had become more evident to me that there is a basic thread that runs through all humanity, connecting us to one another. We were all just trying to find our way.

As we departed, Grandmother Margaret gave each of us a big, warm hug and emboldened us to be joyful in all that we did. Anna and I walked away from the gathering somewhat wistful, got into her car and drove away. We were both silent as we privately recalled the emotional events of the weekend. As we drove down the bumpy, dirt road toward the highway, a large owl spread its wings and flew across our path.

Journal Entry
JANUARY 29, 2010

What will serve a higher purpose? KC or Sedona? What will my guides tell me? How will I learn more about myself? Staying here or moving—what do my guides tell me? What does my heart tell me? Can I live in Sedona and feel fulfilled? I would have lots of time for reflection, music, reading. Am I attached here in KC? Do I need to detach? In my heart I know I have to detach in order to attach to new ideas, new ways—this will not be done here. I have done my work here; now it's time to move to the next phase. I need reflection time, time to explore; this must be done by ME. Seeds will germinate and sprout, but they must be fertilized with enthusiasm and fresh ideas. Give yourself two years to settle and learn. New locations are good to keep you stimulated. There is much to learn, to explore.

26
THE GRANDMOTHER EFFECT

The three Grandmothers, whom I had the great fortune to meet, had such a profound impact on how I was to evolve. I believe something had shifted in me and I was ready to start truly living again. Therefore, I was even more open to new ideas and concepts. It's interesting that when I reached that point, experiences organically flowed into my life, and each and everyone helped me along my journey. There is much truth in the saying, "When the student is ready, the teacher arrives." When you go through an incredible trauma like I did, it breaks open a part of either your heart or mind, or both, and you start on a road to find yourself and reclaim who you are. I had been thriving as part of a couple for 17 years, then suddenly, it was just me again. I had to learn to be alone, learn to make decisions on my own, and move forward without my partner. It was a matter of rediscovering who I was.

The Grandmothers had all endured extraordinary challenges in their lives; I had such tremendous respect for what they had gone through. It helped me to put my loss into perspective and grasp the fact that I too could prevail. Most of the Grandmothers were in their 80s and yet they were still willing to travel the planet, committed to bringing their message of peace, harmony, and love to all. They had a higher purpose—something I longed for.

As I spent time with them, I realized that I had a deep appreciation and fondness for older women. It was a privilege to be in their presence. The depth of their knowledge and wisdom tapped into a source far greater than my awareness. Perhaps it was the essence of the divine feminine; I wasn't sure. All I knew was that they were incredible, exceptional human beings. They had birthed and raised children, literally and figuratively, and exuded a maternal love that was all-encompassing, all-inclusive. I was completely drawn to their pure energy.

The Grandmothers demonstrated that it was possible to live fully, despite the reality of tragedy and grief. They lived completely in the moment, taking each other in, experiencing happiness, and delighting in people. I felt great joy as I settled into their fold.

I had established a lovely community of spiritually-minded people in Kansas City and I loved living near Meredith, Blaine, and the kids. But after about two years, I felt a tug to go back to Sedona. I knew I had to handle some business there, things that I had been avoiding. Mickey and I had an acre of land where we had planned to build a house. We also had a condo. It was foolish to carry two mortgages and pay rent as well. The moment had come for me to figure out what I was going to do with those properties, and what I wanted to do with the rest of my life.

I felt as though I was free-falling, which made me uncomfortable. I liked to plan things out, discuss options. Mickey and I had been a great team in that regard, but that was the point; we were a team. Making decisions of such magnitude on my own had always been somewhat intimidating to me. I had always looked outside of myself for resolution, but was reminded that I now had a new set of tools available to me. I had learned the miraculous benefit of looking within.

I had weathered the greatest of storms and emerged from the depths of despair to embrace life once again. Every occasion that I had to take a step on my own helped to fortify my confidence. The thought of friends I had made, and mentors I had come across, lifted me. And perhaps, most importantly, I felt the support of the Universe. How things would unfold was a mystery to me, but it was a risk I felt empowered to take.

In the annals of time, Mickey and I had created a rich story of our days in Sedona—a story of love and hardship, of shattered dreams and dreams come true. I was aware that I might call on the past to draw on its wisdom, while looking forward to the promise of things to come. But there is an exquisite beauty to wiping a slate clean. It was time for me to take charge. It was time for me to write my own story.

Journal Entry
MAY 28, 2010

Last night in Kansas City. Tough saying goodbye to Meredith. It's then that I wonder if it's all worth it. The ache is so great. I came home, walked Zuni—tearful and bent. Heavy load. It's another little step away and into my own life. Full moon, new beginnings. I'll have to see it in the morning because it wasn't up when I walked Zuni.

I wonder why we pull ourselves away from a good life. I hate when the restless feeling comes on. I'm always trying to learn and improve, so I get restless. I don't think I'll ever feel "settled" because then I become stagnant and don't grow. I'll have to keep calm and do what is right for me.

CONCLUSION

I often reflect upon what I've learned from the devastation of losing Mickey. One thing that I've found is that intensely deep emotions can propel you along many avenues. There is often a freedom that lends itself to feeling bereft. Suddenly, not caring about anything or anyone, allows you to have clarity—you begin to see who you are and what you want. Your walls may come tumbling down, your borders become less defined, and a softness may ensue. A persistent search for answers to questions that have none motivates you to look beyond yourself and the world you have known. You've already said goodbye to your comfort zone—nothing is as it was, so why not push the boundaries a little further? It's as if you must lose control, in order to gain control.

For me, my void was filled with the joy of my relationships, firstly, with my step-kids and grandkids. I can look into their faces and see glimpses of the man I love shining through–the many wonderful, nuanced qualities of Mickey. I have observed Craig and Meredith expand in their marriages and raise incredible children. And I have watched the grandchildren grow into exceptional young adults. If I ever start to slip into despair, I remind myself that Mickey will always be very much alive in them.

Secondly, my chosen family has been a phenomenal, welcome surprise. I could say that I found an alternative path to get through my grief. But, in actuality, it found me. A squad of human angels gathered around to lead me where I needed to go: astrologers, mediums, psychics, intuitives, and friends that I made along my journey. All I needed to do was say yes.

Although it's been fifteen years since Mickey's death, I have a visceral memory of what a challenging time it was during the months and years that followed. There were moments in which I contemplated an easy out: climbing into a bottle, using drugs, even ending my life—anything that would help to alleviate the pain. I was angry, sad, and depressed and I couldn't see any way out. But I came to realize that there is always a way out.

I still get emotional thinking about my beloved Mickey. And even though the anger has subsided, I will always feel that the world has been cheated out of knowing the depth of this beautiful man. But hurting myself would have been the last thing that Mickey would have wanted. He would want me to live with purpose, experience the continuation of what we had created together and be a witness to the wonder of life.

In the same manner that I looked toward others for wisdom, I hope that the words on these pages resonate with some of you who are grieving. Day by day, you will find your way through your anguish—if you stay open to possibilities. And in doing so, you will help others, and they in turn will pass on your wisdom. That's who we are as human beings. We don't live in separate bubbles. We are part of a shared existence.

My path is only my path; it is not for everyone. You must find your own road to renewal. But I strongly encourage you not to limit yourself. Take risks, free your heart, and open your mind. Accept your emotions; be kind to yourself. Don't feel like you must be, or act in a certain way that will make others feel more comfortable. It is your time. Talk to a professional, journal, meditate, pray, exercise—whatever you need to do to get through.

I truly believe that the Universe is beneficent and has a plan for all of us. Happiness and success are our birthrights. Teachers are all around us if we are awake enough to take notice. I have found a strength in me since Mickey passed. I have more confidence and I'm not afraid to make mistakes. I take care of myself in a myriad of ways and I find joy in helping others who are wrestling with loss. That is the reason I wrote this book. If it benefits anyone, then it's been well worth it.

I feel a great deal of gratitude to my family and friends and all the healers and teachers with whom I have journeyed. They have helped me to find my center, stand in my power, and know myself, so that I could be who I always needed to be—Just Me.

*** THE END ***

This picture is of Mickey and me right after we got married.

It shows the happiness, hopes and dreams we had for a long and prosperous future together.

Ingram Content Group UK Ltd.
Milton Keynes UK
UKHW010648050623
422889UK00005B/925